The World of Pompeii

The World of Pompeii

Text by **Aldo Massa**

Translated by David McDougall

Minerva

Contents

Cover pages: A street in Pompeii.
Frontispiece: The Doric portico of the Pompeii forum, with Vesuvius in the background.

1 - A city out of antiquity

We can learn a great deal about how a people lived by looking at the places it lived in. Naples and Pompeii are set in a region of magnificent natural beauty, richly endowed by history, myth and religion. We can visit Patria with Scipio, Baiae with Horace, Elysium with Virgil, Puozzoli with Saint Paul, Cumae with the Sybil, and Misenum with Pliny the Younger—who was a witness of one of the greatest disasters in history, a catastrophe which destroyed three towns and killed Pliny the Elder.

Here we are in Pompeii, a city obliterated in one day by lava erupting from nearby Vesuvius.

The streets, which once echoed to the sounds of its forty thousand inhabitants, are empty now, but they are lit by the same blazing sun, and the silence is filled with memories. Here are the tracks of the last carts to run over these roads; here are the fountains and triumphal arches which adorned the city. Come into one of the food shops—that bread was baked on 23rd November 79! We can study the patterns of everyday trade in a town out of antiquity. Let us walk along the Street of Tombs—a road which seems so appropriate in a town which was once whole before it suddenly disappeared in a vast grave.

We shall visit houses where we shall try to find things as the last owners left them. We shall be seeking to reconstruct the way of life of the people who lived there—who must have left traces of their personality in their dwellings, empty since they departed. The workshop full of unfinished objects and strange tools teaches us that we must give the ancient world credit for several inventions which we thought were modern. *Nova inventa antiqua.* The *ergastulum* still speaks to us of the miseries of the slave. The sumptuous apartments of the Roman citizen prove to us that he often understood better than we the pleasures of life. We shall rediscover the details of the dress and elegance of the Pompeian lady from a thousand jewels, mirrors and caskets. Finally we shall join our hosts on the couches of the *triclinium* for a magnificent feast from the pages of Lucullus, whose contemporaries used to holiday in Pompeii. We can discover the menu of a dinner whose remains are still preserved—a dinner interrupted by Vesuvius!

Enough of the structure of the forum, the basilica and the temples remains for the eye to be able to appreciate how they used to be. Here we can compare the classical style of the original buildings with the impurities of later alterations. And here we shall discover details of public and religious life in Roman times which confirm history, or fill in the gaps it has left.

On the *album* of the streets and the marble of the tombs, on the walls of houses and public buildings, we can make out lines from Ovid and Virgil. We read posters advertising circuses, slogans from political campaigns, slaves' protests, cries from the heart, fine classical verses, expressions in vulgar speech,

with their mistakes and individual spelling. We look around for the men who have traced these lines, which time does not seem to have the power to erase. But the heart which inspired those love poems and the hand which wrote them have been dead for centuries. The Pompeians themselves are cast in the hardened lava; they appear before us in plaster statues, silent, in the appalling contortions of their deaths.

Pompeii, dedicated to Venus, was a town of pleasure. Its attractions brought the Roman great, who liked to own villas there. They lived exceedingly well, and we remember the splendours of the baths, where they spent a large part of their days and nights, and the performances at the theatres and amphitheatres, the posters and admission tickets for which tell us about the spectacles which were being presented.

How much the Pompeians valued intellectual pleasures, how they applauded Aeschylus, Plautus, and all the masterpieces of Greece and Rome! But how much were violent emotions a part of the personality of this pleasure-loving and cruel people, who enjoyed watching the spectacle of human agony, and who, deaf to the gladiator's pleas, condemned him pitilessly to see a man die nobly!

Snow-topped volcanoes are not unknown. Vesuvius occasionally has a mantle of hoarfrost, and in 1819 snow was discovered under currents of lava which had buried it for centuries. Strabo attributes the special

"The streets, which once echoed to the sounds of its forty thousand inhabitants, are empty today, but they are lit by the same blazing sun, and the silence is filled with memories."—Pompeii, Street of Plenty.

fertility of the Pompeian soil to the volcanic ash which is its principal component.

No one should be surprised that Pompeii should have grown up so near such a terrible neighbour as Vesuvius. On the very edge of this fearful mountain there are still today two sizable communities: Torre del Greco and Torre dell'Annunziata. The inhabitants have had numerous warnings. They know that their ancestors have often been overwhelmed by eruptions of lava, and yet they sleep peacefully on the edge of the volcano. Torrents of flame do not frighten them, though danger may scatter them from time to time; but no sooner has the lava hardened than the richness of nature calls them back to the ancestral fields, which are fertile and inviting.

Pompeii is four miles from the crater of Vesuvius, and fourteen miles from Naples.

Campania was inhabited by the Oscans, who claimed to be the original inhabitants, confusing themselves with the ancient *Ausonii.* Visited by Phoenicians and Greeks, who brought an advanced civilisation, later living under the influence of the Etruscans, who extended their conquests as far as these fertile lands, they were finally conquered, not without resistance, by Rome, which imposed its language and customs. Pompeii became a Roman municipality. An historian explains: "The municipalities were the towns of conquered lands. As a mark of special favour, Rome granted them the rights of Roman cities—a magnificent gift, constantly recalled

by their very name, which derives from *munus,* gift. Their constitutions, which were fairly similar to those of the Roman colonies, were primarily based on that of the metropolis." The town of Pompeii was composed of three orders: senators, knights, people.

The municipal administration consisted of an *Aedile,* two *Duoviri* who were responsible for justice, the *Praetor,* the *Censor,* the *Quaestor,* the administrator of the public treasury, the town's patron, the leaders of the suburbs, and a hundred *Decuriones,* who made up the great council. In Rome the *Decuriones* were called Senators.

Trade with Africa, the East and distant lands brought great wealth to Pompeii. Livy and Florus tell us that its harbour was magnificent.

What a superb situation! Near Naples, which sent illustrious visitors, near the volcano which made the surrounding fields fertile, the town spread from the height of its rock of lava to the edge of the sea. From the terraces of their houses, ranged like the steps of an amphitheatre, the Pompeians could make out, at the same time, fertile fields, a sparkling sea, the Gulf of Stabiae, the shores of Sorrento, the Isle of Capri, Mount Pausilippus, Naples and Vesuvius! Florus claims that it was the finest spot not only in Italy, but in all the world.

The Emperor Claudius was a frequent visitor. Cicero wrote several works in the town, particularly his treatise *De Officiis.* Phaedrus wrote his fables here.

"Entry to the town was through a series of large gates. Nola gate is well preserved."
Below: Photograph of Nola gate and a tomb. Right: Bronze statue, from Pompeii.

2 - A tour of the town

From its appearance it is generally agreed that the town had a population of forty thousand; its ships, which brought it riches from the East, also brought great artists from Greece.

Pompeii had numerous monuments. From the civil forum to the barracks there are several temples, a basilica, three squares, the tomb of Eumachia, the baths, two theatres, a great many shops and nearly a thousand marble columns.

The town was surrounded by walls, except on the sea side. They formed a double rampart with a terrace wide enough for three chariots to ride abreast. This must have been a superb promenade from which to enjoy the view and the sea air. The walls are flanked at regular intervals by large square towers; these were damaged several times by war and the volcano, and show signs of restoration at different times.

Entry to the town was through a series of large gates. Nola gate is well preserved; Herculaneum gate very old. The main entrance is protected by arrow slits for archers. Roman roads led to each of the gates.

The streets are better paved and kept up than they were in a number of European cities at the beginning of this century. The pavements, *margines,* are made of asphalt; the roadway, *agger,* was of course used for drainage; the tracks of carriage wheels are still visible, particularly the heavy *plaustrum,* which was drawn by oxen. Stepping stones,

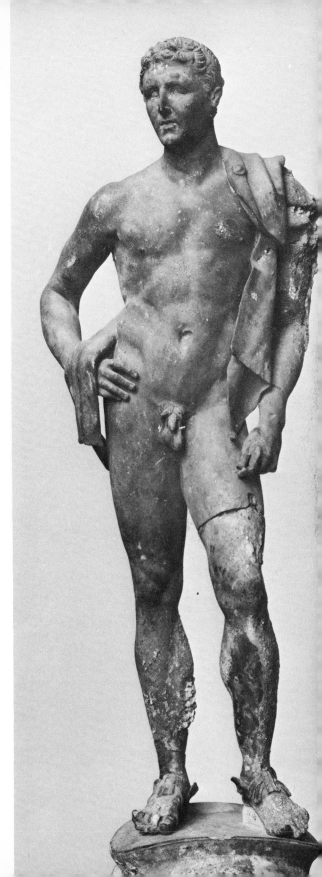

"The streets are very narrow... Tracks left by carriage wheels are still visible in the roadway... Stepping stones, forming paths accross the roadway, allowed the Pompeian lady to pass from one pavement to another without dirtying her feet... The ruins, sad and empty today, once reverberated with noises as lively as those made by a modern Neapolitan crowd."

forming paths across the roadway, allowed the Pompeian lady to pass from one pavement to another without dirtying her feet.

The roads are very narrow; they are never more than 21 feet wide, and are often only 12.

The sewers are carefully concealed beneath the pavements; they lead to a sea outlet.

There were numerous fine fountains, and wells have been found. The abundance of fresh, limpid water at a height exposed to the burning sun must have been particularly valued.

The town contains a number of impressive monuments. Thus at a *quadrivium,* a crossroads of the Forum, Mercury and Temple Streets, there are marble-clad triumphal arches, topped by statues.

The houses appear to have been newly built. The town had once already been engulfed by Vesuvius, and reconstruction had hardly been completed before it was completely destroyed. The interiors of their buildings were architecturally more important for the Pompeians than the façades. The houses are generally not high; they are normally two storeys, rarely three. They have all lost their roofs. The volcano destroyed the fine terraces covered with creeping vines, flowers and colonnades.

The ruins, sad and empty today, once reverberated with noises as lively as those made by a modern Neapolitan crowd. The streets rang with an enormous variety of cries. The stall-holder was not prepared simply to display his merchandise; he hawked it at the

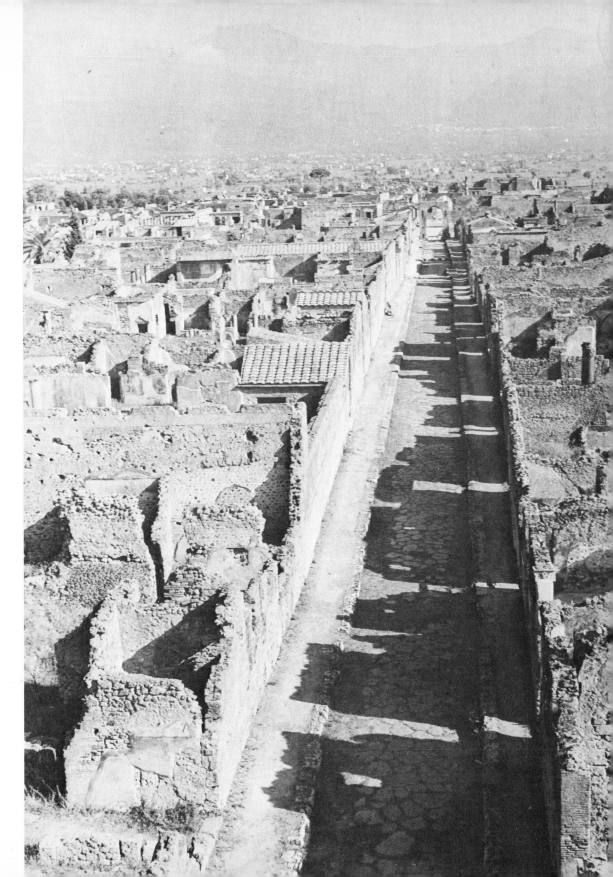

top of his voice, trying to capture the passing trade with the cheapness of his prices.

The wine merchant would attract attention by shaking an ivy branch; the butcher held a myrtle branch, to show that his meats came from the mountains, where the myrtle grows.

Each street seller had his own cry. Business went to the man who shouted loudest, without worrying what happened to the ears of the passers-by. One has to have visited the region to gain some idea of the mimicry and quick movements of the Neapolitans, whose gestures are always accompanied by an inexhaustible supply of words.

But here is the *accensus,* whose job is to announce the time. The sundial shows that it is the sixth hour, noon; the heat of the sun makes it necessary to rest; it is time for the siesta. Everything closes down to open again later.

The walls were covered with murals. There are symbolic serpents, *lares vitales et comitales,* protectors of streets and suburbs. The shops, which were unnumbered, carried trade signs. A chemist was represented by a snake in coils eating a pine cone. Butchers displayed an ox, dairies a goat, millers a mill turned by an ass, wine merchants a jar carried on poles by two men. A priest leading a bull to the altar and figures perfuming a corpse were the sign of a *mycolium,* the shop which sold perfumes and scents for funerals and sacrifices. And above the doors of the *thermopoles,* which were the Roman equivalent of the café or public house, was a very moral picture; Ulysses rejecting Circë's potion.

Sometimes, when the old sign is missing, articles found in the shop tell us what its use was. This must have been a barber's shop—here are the niches where he put his vases of toilet water, here is the stone stool where his clients sat. This was a smithy. The workshop, whose master has been gone for so many centuries, still contains his forge, only slightly damaged, his tools, his hammers, his horse-shoes.

This shop belonged to a grocer and oil merchant. The counter is made of onion marble and worn sandstone. Between two elegant rose windows we notice a slab of green porphyry. Here are nine really beautiful terracotta and bronze jars; we almost expect to find that they still contain soft clammy olives. The oil was pressed in a cement-clad cellar, as is still the custom in Italy. Cato tells us that Pompeii was famous for its presses and mills. The hand mills look very like models that are still found in certain countries. The upper millstone was turned over the lower by means of a wooden staff pushed by a slave or an ass.

In one bakery the dough was ready for the oven. In another, everything was in its place: the mill to grind the wheat, the jars to take the flour, the vases to pour the water, the brasier to light the fire. Eighty loaves were taken from a hermetically sealed oven; they had been put there on 23rd November 79! They were so well preserved that it has been possible to analyse them chemically.

Artist's impression and cross-section of the walls of Pompeii. This reconstruction, like several others in the book, is the work of Mazois, the French architect and archaeologist, who spent three years in Pompeii.

They are not very big; their shapes are charming. A painting tells us that bread was sold on stalls on the streets. There were a great many bakers; the owners sent their wheat to have it turned into bread. The police enforced strict quality standards and required brand marks to be shown.

Some of the loaves read *siglio granii,* wheaten flour, and others *e cicere,* chick-pea flour. These words were engraved with typeface characters. It seems strange that the Romans should have understood the use of such characters in this limited context, and that is should have taken so many centuries to progress from this invention to printing, which appears to be based on the same principle.

One of the finest streets, set with spectacular monuments, is the Street of Tombs.

The Romans generally thought of death with neither fear nor hope. They sought to become familiar with it; it was represented at their feats and festivals. The presence of death was an encouragement to enjoy life, and not put off till the morrow pleasures which they would later perhaps not be able to enjoy.

Entering the town by Herculaneum gate, at a charming and popular spot, the visitor passes superb tombs on both sides of the street. The Romans made their tombs look as magnificent as everything else they built.

The tombs do not compare with those which are still one of the wonders of Rome. They are smaller; but they are better preserved. They are remarkable, particularly, for the exquisite elegance of their decoration.

The tombs are frequently striking for their stucco embellishments, for the beauty of the pilasters, columns, bas-reliefs and statues. Some of the crypts have fine marble doorways. The mausoleum of Cneius and Labo is decorated with statues of a man wearing a toga and a heavily shrouded woman.

Sometimes the sculpture adds a commentary to the epitaph. The *bisellium* was awarded as a mark of great honour. It was a seat large enough for two people, but used by only one—who was consequently especially comfortable. The owner had the right to be carried by slaves during public festivals. It was a privilege greatly sought by the Pompeians, as they tell us from their tombs.

Some of the bas-reliefs show interesting scenes from the Roman way of life. The most curious details of gladiatorial bouts are provided by sculptures on Scaurus's tomb.

Naevolia's monument to Munatius depicts the Augustal's funeral ceremony. A young priest, Camillus, places the urn on the altar. A standing child appears to be the dead man's son. On the right of the tableau the *Decuriones,* officers of the municipality, and the *Sexviri Augustales,* wearing their special togas, honour their dead colleague. On the left, men, women and children, carrying baskets of flowers, face the altar. A charming young girl, Naevolia, comes forward to say a last farewell to someone she loved—though what the relationship was between them is not clear.

"Cato tells us that Pompeii was famous for its presses and oil mills."
Left: Remains of a shop with oil vases.

Opposite: Sundial in the garden of "the gilded joys"; grooves for a sliding door, and hinges from a shop on Nola Street.

Right: weights and scales from Pompeii, in the Naples museum.

"Eighty loaves were taken from a hermetically sealed oven; they were put there on 23rd November 79." Opposite: Reconstruction of the bakery, by Mazois, and photographs of the millstone and a phallic symbol on the wall of the shop.

Several tombs feature *praeficae* and *bustuariae,* women paid in one case to sing the dead man's praise, in the other to weep for him.

One bas-relief has given rise to some controversy. It represents a ship sailing in a stormy sea. At the captain's command the sails are being taken in by spirits as the boat enters port; the figurehead represents Minerva.

Clearly, this scene symbolizes the last moments of life. For some, it shows wisdom preceding the boat, which, having passed through a sea strewn with reefs, has reached the port of peace and no longer needs oars or sails to combat the elements. A rival explanation is more prosaic. The boat only signifies that the deceased made his fortune from sea trade.

To prove that the boat was the symbol of life arriving at the port of eternal rest, one historian cites early Christian tombstones. But there are great differences between the ideology of the town of Venus and that of the Catacombs. We should turn to pagan authors for explanations of pagan things. "I want the ships you sculpt on my tomb to be at full sail", Petronius makes a merchant tell Trimalchio, "I should be seated on a tribunal, wearing the magistral toga. By my side should be a large sack of coins to distribute to the people." (Sat. 16.) This is the real spirit of paganism; to be represented after death by the arrogant display of honours and wealth accumulated during life!

"Entering the town by Herculaneum gate, at a charming and popular spot, the visitor passes superb tombs on both sides of the street."—Opposite: Photograph of the Street of Tombs seen from Herculaneum gate. Right: Map.

The form of the tomb varied according to the sculptor's taste. That of Cerrinus is made to look like a sentry box. This shows us that the dead man was a soldier—a brave man who stood courageously at his post.

The tombs of children were normally covered with flowers. Children aged nine or younger were buried. It was forbidden to burn them on the funeral pyre, as was also the case for people who had been struck by lightning.

The rooms of the crypt were sometimes lit by wall vents, and sometimes by a lamp hanging in the vault. The urn containing the ashes is sometimes extremely simple: it is placed in a niche in the stonework. There are also urns which are so ornate and so exquisitely beautiful that they defy modern artists to produce anything finer. I am thinking particularly of a magnificent vase in oriental alabaster, and especially of an urn in the shape of an elegant amphora; a blue glass vessel covered with a relief enamel paste with vine branches and scenes of the wine harvest.

In the famous tomb consecrated by Naevolia three hermetically sealed glass urns were found, clad in lead envelopes. The remains they contained were still preserved in a mixture of wine, water and oil.

The dying Christian asked for the prayers of those he had loved; Tibullus requested Neëra and his mother to cover his ashes with milk and old wine!

The *sepulcretum*, enclosed by a wall,

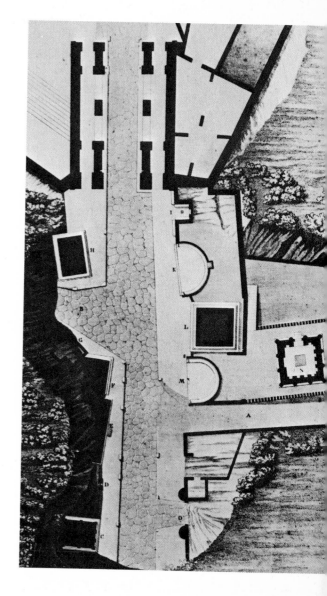

contained flat stones on which offerings were placed. In a vault belonging to the Nistacidia family a vase embedded in the ground was designed for libations or flowers.

An enclosure within the vault about 18 feet square is strewn with small *cippi* shaped like heads; these were the *columellae,* decorated with female herms with braided hair.

The funerals of the rich were celebrated with a pomp which has often been described, but the poor and the slaves died as they had lived, unknown and despised. There were no cypress branches hanging over the entrances to their crypts; no rare scents were scattered over their funeral pyres—only a little pitch to stoke up the flames. If there had been many deaths in an epidemic, several bodies would be heaped up together to be burned at the same time. Following an ancient Roman prejudice, women's bodies were placed beneath those of the men, in the belief that the flames would take better.

Clearly a single pauper would not be entitled to an individual tomb. The great built vast rooms for their slaves and freedmen, the walls set with curved niches like those where pigeons nest; they were consequently called *columbaria,* dovecots. The niches were systematically arranged in layers; the funeral urns were placed in them.

In the tomb of Tycheus a bench and two rows of niches designed for urns extend along the walls.

The Pompeians knew that with death they lost all their worldly goods. They could retain

only one property; their tomb, which often bears the letter H.M.H.N.S.: *Hoc monumentum haeredis non sequatur,* this monument cannot be inherited by the heirs.

We are now entering a superb *triclinium* on the Street of Tombs. The *triclinium* was the room where the *silicernia* or *novemdialia*—feasts in honour of the dead—were celebrated. The one we are visiting in Pompeii is very different from a Christian chapel of rest. The walls are decorated with charming paintings of animals, birds and flowers; three inclined couches are set around a table. A little imagination can give back the couches their soft cushions, and its luxurious coverings to the table. The remains of a sacrifice offered to the infernal deities could not be left. In a sepulchral but graceful boudoir, the friends of the deceased, spread out at their ease, celebrated their mourning with an excellent dinner, where fine wine flowed at least as amply as tears. The dinner began with shell-

"The form of the tomb varied according to the sculptor's taste..." Opposite: Two Pompeian tombs.

25

fish, which was traditional at funerals, and continued with more lavish dishes. The guests ended their meal by drinking so much that they would have been sad indeed if Bacchus had not succeeded in procuring forgetfulness for their unhappiness.

In the middle of the line of tombs on Herculaneum Street is a covered hemicycle. It is a niche topped by a cul-de-four, decorated in stucco, and set with charming paintings, with benches raised on two steps running round the walls. Visitors to the Street of Tombs came to rest on these benches. After talking about the deceased, their conversation would turn to other things. This was where the great orator came with Scaevola the augur; *In hemicyclo sedente ut solebat,* he tells us himself in his introduction to his treatise *De Amicitia.*

In this place, where so many monuments of his time are still standing, Cicero would find himself at home if he were to return. As we sit on the very stone where this great man sat, we evoke his memory. We can see him arriving from Rome; the crowd gathers around him, and people embrace him in the Roman manner, eager to question him. Understanding all the great problems of the age, adept in all the sciences, he more than any other can talk of so many things likely to interest them. His eloquence, which he cannot restrain, reaches extraordinary heights as it is fed by the crowd's applause. And when he encounters opposition, his irritation enables him to give off sparks of his most

brilliant genius. It was on this spot, at sunset under a cloudless sky, that he prepared his most famous pieces as he talked to his friends.

People came a long way to hear him, and the world's great would come to visit him. It was to this hemicycle, sitting beside him perhaps, that Augustus would come to ask for his support against Antony.

Cicero had houses in and around Pompeii. He tells us that one day Julius Caesar came to ask his hospitality. He was flattered to receive him, but he found the occasion onerous, because the Master of the Earth was accompanied by so many retainers. Admitting that he was proud to have received such a visit, he would say that he hoped it would not be repeated. "Once is enough. *Semel satis est;* so powerful a man cannot be a friend to whom one can say: "I should be pleased to see you whenever you are passing."

"This is a superb triclinium. This triclinium was the room where feasts in honour of the dead were held... The dinner began with shell-fish, and continued with more lavish dishes." Below: Artist's impression of the triclinium, and reconstruction of a tomb, by Mazois.

Opposite: Inscription on a tomb sited by Nola gate.

3. Life and society

Houses in Pompeii are surprisingly small. Wealthy citizens spent most of their time away from home.

Seen from the street, the façades are not at all striking. All windows gave onto the courtyard and gardens. There are no chimneystacks. The midday sun is bright in Italy, but it does not guarantee eternal Spring. During the winter the Pompeians, like the Greeks before them, used brasiers *(camini portatiles)*.

All the houses look remarkably similar. However, some are strikingly elegant, like Sallust's house; others are particularly large, like Pansa's; others especially tall, like Diomedes's. Let us take a closer look at the second of these.

The house opens onto three streets, where the ground floor was occupied by shops. Here, too, were the rented apartments. To be an *inquilinus,* tenant, was then considered somewhat humiliating. Dionysius of Halicarnassus tells us that the less well-off used to join in cooperatives to build houses as a joint venture. One would own the ground floor; another the second; yet another the third. Cicero, who owned twenty houses, was quite prepared to make a profit from his properties. It was not well thought of to be a lodgings keeper—*civile inquilinus*—and Cataline used the epithet as a jibe against Cicero. Rich citizens had a slave—*servus insularus*—who was responsible for lettings. An *insula* was a group of buildings surrounded by streets, like an island surrounded by water.

Doorway of a house on the Street of Plenty. The body of the door has been based on a mould made from the hollow left in the volcanic lava by the wood of the original door after the destruction of Pompeii. The bronze work is original. "The first courtyard is rectangular, surrounded by porticos and columns: this is the atrium." Below: The atrium of the house of the Vettii.

The door of Pansa's residence no longer exists. All the solid oak doors in Pompeii have disappeared with their gilded nails, their knockers and bells. We know them only from the wall-paintings—fragile frescos which have better withstood the volcano than iron and steel.

The door had a particular importance for the Romans. It was decorated with elegant sculptures, it was carefully lit and garlanded on feast days. The door was a sacred object, protected by four deities: Janus was guardian of the whole, *janua*; Forculus was responsible for the cornice, *fores*; Limentius for the threshold, *limen*; Cardea for the hinges, *cardines*.

At the main entry is the lobby or *prothyrum*. It was here that the images of the *lares*, or household gods, were placed. On the inner wall is a painting of a serpent or custodial deity, guardian of the home. On one side is a lamp burning in his honour; the brick ledge which supported it is still attached to the wall.

The porter was a slave; his feelings were of no account. To prevent him from leaving to gossip with the neighbours, a long chain was attached to his foot. He would ask each visitor his name before announcing it *(Quis tu?)*. As the guest entered his feet crossed a graceful mosaic, which offered, as a greeting, the word *Salve*, welcome.

The guard dog at the porter's side was less welcoming. A superb Pompeian mosaic shows a large dog ready to spring; it is res-trained by a chain. Beneath the picture, in fine characters, we read the words: *Cave canem!* beware of the dog.

The recalls a passage from Petronius. "At the entrance", he writes "was a porter dressed in green, with a cherry red belt, who was shelling peas into a silver basin. Over the doorway there hung a golden cage, which housed a brightly plumaged magpie, whose song welcomed guests to the house. Stunned by all these things, I nearly fell over—and would probably have broken a leg—when I saw the dog painted on the left-hand wall near the porter's lodge. It was on a chain, and beneath it were the words: *Cave canem!* It made us laugh."

The first courtyard is rectangular, surrounded by porticos and columns: this is the *atrium*. The small bedrooms, lit only from their doorways, housed the guests *(hospitia)* and the slaves *(ergastula)*.

In the middle of the courtyard was the *impluvium*, a large reservoir which collected storm water falling through the *compluvium*, an opening in the ceiling designed to let in rain water.

Long galleries *(alae)* were lined with seats which were set apart for dependents and clients. To escape them, and perhaps for other reasons, the master of the house kept a key to the back door *(posticium)*. At the end of the *atrium* are corridors *(fauces)* and various rooms, particularly the *tablinum*, a library where paintings of the ancestors and family records were kept.

The books were kept in cedar chests (*armoria*). Their size was similar to our octavo. Their covers were brightly coloured, while pumice-stone and oil of cedar gave their leaves an attractive finish. As in our own time, *risqué* books were not the least read in the library; but once they had lost the attraction of scandal and novelty, would be the first to be consigned to the wastepaper basket.

The second courtyard, or peristyle, was the most ornate part of the house. Beneath porticos decorated with paintings, supported by marble columns, embellished by statues, encircled by vases filled with flowers, we find the master's apartments: the *cubicula*, bedrooms, the *aecus*, drawing room, and the *venereum*, a room which has greatly intrigued some historians, probably a boudoir.

In the middle of the peristyle is a fountain, on a parapet where sculptor and architect have competed in elegance and good taste. The water flowing from this fountain fell into rich basins from where it splashed in gushes sparkling in the sun. Around the fountain are statues and charming vases.

In the courtyard, beyond beds planted with the rarest and most brightly coloured flowers, was the vegetable garden. Vesuvius has preserved the layout of the borders beneath a layer of ash.

The collapse of the ceilings makes it difficult to be sure about the make-up of the upper storeys. This must have been the *gynaeceum*, or women's apartments.

The roofing was generally covered by terraces; this one was the *solarium*. During winter one could amble in the gentle heat of the sun; in summer one could find shade behind climbing vines and potted plants, or beneath red-dyed veils—called *courtinae*, because they were invented in a courtyard—one belonging to Attalus, king of Pergamum.

The houses of Pompeii are empty; one would think that the inhabitants had taken all their furniture with them; in fact, there are many examples in the Naples museum.

The empty cubicles still contain the great slabs of stone which were the Pompeians' beds. On this somewhat hard couch were placed soft mattresses, bolsters and feather pillows. Fine sheets were greatly valued, but the supreme luxury was the counterpane. Martial tells us that a favourite colour was purple, fringed with rich furs.

Trestle beds very like those of our time have been found; they are in bronze or highly finished wood. No curtains have survived; the only trace of them are the metal rings from which they hung.

But there is no need to catalogue the chandeliers, candelabra, vases, and all the enormous variety of household objects and pieces of furniture that have been discovered. These things are familiar to most of us.

Let us try to recreate in our imagination the daily life of the inhabitants of these deserted houses. How did the Pompeians live—slaves, masters, women?

In antiquity the slave was considered to be of a different nature to a free man, as though

In the middle of the courtyard was the impluvium, a large reservoir which collected storm water falling through the compluvium, an opening in the ceiling designed to let in rain water." Left: Photograph of the impluvium in the house of Lucretia and cross-section reconstruction.

Two bronze frying-pans, from Pompeii. Below right: Vase from the house of an aristocrat.

Above: Atrium of the house of Caius Secundus.

he belonged to another human species. He was the property of his master; an animate tool. Roman law saw him as a being inferior to man, with no legal rights, and comparable to the basest animal. The slave had no family; he was not allowed the consolation of prayer, for the gods despised such unworthy devotions. Cato reserved the right to make religious observance to the master alone.

The lot of the slave was to suffer all imaginable indignities and discomforts to provide the free citizen with the pleasures of life. He was expected to perform all duties—the highest and the lowest. His rôle was to spare his master every exertion—even intellectual effort. Seneca tells us that Calvitius paid 100,000 sesterces each for eleven slaves. One of them knew all Homer by heart; others knew Hesiod and the leading lyrists. He would make them stand by his couch as he ate. They would whisper quotations to him—which he himself would not have been able to repeat without appalling mistakes.

Slaves were sold at every price, from the lowest. Slaves could be bought in the market-place for very little. They were assigned the most menial tasks. While some, like Plautus and Terence, charmed their masters with their verses and their wit, others would share with the ass the humble task of turning the grindstone in the mill. Plautus himself was apparently sometimes ordered to turn the millstone, and he seems to have retained some resentment about being made to perform this dispiriting task, which he often mentions. "Be careful, Davus", one of his characters says, "I shall give you a good thrashing, and then send you to work the mill. And I swear that I shall take your place at the grindstone before I let you leave it."

The wealthy citizen boosted his self-esteem through owning an enormous number of slaves. We learn from history that as many as twenty thousand could belong to one man. Trimalchio, in Petronius, did not know personally a tenth of his slaves; he was told each morning how many had been born the previous night. Seneca tells us of a freedman who had so many slaves that he employed a secretary to keep track of the changes in numbers which took place each day through sales, births and deaths. Greece supplied intellectuals, Asia cooks, Africa runners, Germany gladiators. It would have cost a great deal to feed and clothe so many people adequately. Apuleius tells us that slaves were branded with a letter on their foreheads; their hair was shaved on one side of their heads, and they wore an iron ring on their ankles. They were dressed in filthy rags, and their badly fed bodies, weakened by overwork and continual beatings, looked revoltingly ill-nourished.

The Digest mentions the *vicarius,* or slave's substitute. What a dreadful fate to be a slave's slave! There could be nothing worse, except perhaps to be the slave of a capricious mistress. Thus Juvenal: "Have a cross prepared for this slave.—What crime has he committed? Where are the witnesses? Who de-

"The houses of Pompeii are empty; one would think that the inhabitants had taken all their furniture with them; in fact, there are many examples in the Naples museum." This Pompeian chest is one of many exhibits in the museum.

Below: Reconstruction of the "house of the tragic poet" by the English architect William Gell.

Right: The house of Cornelius Tegeatus, or "house of the Ephebe".

Following pages: Fountain from the "house of the large fountain", on the Street of Mercury. The masks are in marble, and imported from Egypt.

"The second courtyard, or peristyle, was the most ornate part of the house."—Left: Reservoir in the peristyle of the house of Meneager. Below: Peristyle from the house of Loreius Tiburtinus.

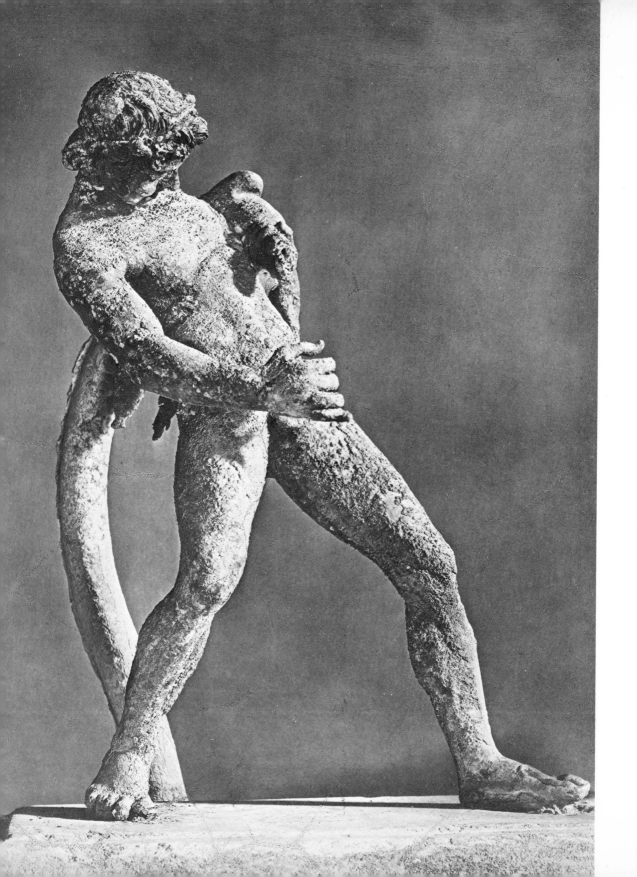

nounced him? We must hear them; it is impossible to take too much time to decide on a man's death.—A man's death? You fool! Is a slave a man? Perhaps he isn't guilty; but he shall die. I have decided; I order it. My will is the law."

How hard a slave had to work to win his freedom! How much sweat and privation, and what effort, to accumulate so little savings! Money boxes have been found in Pompeii which only contained bronze coins— and no doubt they had been painfully put aside one by one. The law did not favour freedom for slaves. It placed obstacles in the way, and was zealous in seeing that they were effective. A master would often go back on his word, and his greed punished his servant for having served him too well.

But was the female slave *(ancilla)* any better off than her male colleague? We shall only discuss the *ornatrix,* or lady's-maid. The Pompeian lady was a decadent shadow of the austere Roman matron of former times. If she had all the caprices of our modern fashionable women, she had more power to tyrannize her servants and impose all her whims on them. The custom of going to circuses, and the attitude she adopted to her slave, made her do things which were natural to her, but which to our eyes appear revolting and barbaric. The *ancilla* whose responsibility it was to dress the hair of a difficult and pretentious woman would often envy the fate of the slave who turned the grindstone with the ass. A hair-pin out of place could mean a box on the ear; and the slave might well be happy if she escaped having her hair pulled, or the torture of being hung up by her hair. To spare herself the effort of striking the girl herself, the matron was assisted by a *carnifex,* tormentor. If an unhappy servant did not succeed in making her mistress look as beautiful as she expected to be, the *carnifex* would seize her, ill-use her, and send her away soundly beaten, saying: "You may go! Justice has been done!" Juvenal tells us that for some masters the swish of the whip was a music sweeter than the song of the sirens.

Happily, all mistresses were not so difficult or so cruel. Gentle Napea deserved Ovid's praise: "Her hair dresser was safe. She was not the sort of woman who would scratch her face or stick pins in her arms." What a compliment!

If the maid had the modesty natural in a young girl, how difficult she would find it to please husband and wife equally. They were often far from agreeing with each other.

The master would make his demands; the mistress had hers as well. The *ancilla* had difficult duties to perform. If she did her work badly, she would be beaten by her mistress. If she did too well, she would be beaten by her master. Amongst the many methods invented by feminine guile for sending love letters, here is one which deserves to be better known. The lady would write in milk on the bare shoulders of her personal slave. It was only necessary to rub a little coal dust over the milk to make the letters visible, and a splash of water obliterated the last traces of this living letter.

What must have been the fashionable districts (near the forum and the theatres) have been thoroughly excavated. But the house of the small tradesman, or even the pauper, can yield even more interesting information, as the history of the common people in antiquity is less well known than that of the wealthier sectors.

The Romans wore the toga, a noble and elegant dress, but one which was easily dirtied. It was a point of honour to keep it clean, and it was often sent to the cleaner's. One such house, called a *fullonica,* is particularly well known; it had all the instruments necessary for cleaning and dyeing; the various stages of the dyeing process were depicted in murals.

Another *fullonica* which has been discovered is very curious. It is in two parts; the workshop and the master's house. It looks as though work in the workshop has just finished. The clothes are ready for washing in the basin; the water taps are in good working order. A room which links the workshop to the house was decorated with fine murals. They include a particularly attractive painting of Venus, who is arranging her hair in a mirror while a cupid holds a perfume-box.

A sculptor's studio is full of blocks of marble—and in one of them the sculptor's chisel is still embedded.

The Romans despised industry and trade.

"The trader", Cicero writes, "who buys goods cheaply to resell dear, only makes a profit through lies and fraud; it is a job which ought to be left to the slave."

Medicine was often a career for slaves and freedmen. In several doctors' and dentists' surgeries drugs and a large quantity of instruments have been discovered which had been believed to be modern inventions; they had been highly developed in Pompeii. Flasks have been discovered in a chemist's shop which still contained medicines.

The free citizen despised everything which he considered slave's work. Amongst his numerous slaves were men who spared him all material worries, and whose only aim in life was to maximize his enjoyment. The Pompeian wore the toga, a cumbersome but impressive dress. He was a solid citizen, and he walked slowly; unlike the slave, whose duties often obliged him to run through the streets.

The citizen found a use for each hour of his day. As he left his house in the morning, he would be met by a crowd of clients, *salutores,* who would cluster around him, embracing him, kissing his hand and running after him. The clients were willing to suffer winter frosts and summer heat while waiting for their master, who would often greet them with no more than a disdainful glance. Their homage had an ulterior motive; they were paid six sesterces each by the great man's treasurer. This institution, which supported a great many paupers, was called

"The dressing ceremony was so important for Roman matrons that Juvenal compares their boudoir to the terrible tribunal of Dionysius the Tyrant.—Below: Example of a Pompeian hair style. Right: Mural from the house of Apollo.

the *sportula.* The wealthy Pompeian would make for the forum, where he would take part in all aspects of public affairs. At noon, he returned to take his siesta with the fountains playing in the background. Life outside would only begin again at two o'clock.

The citizen in any case preferred night to day. He despised sunlight, which shone on the lowest creatures, costing them nothing.

It is evening; the master is at supper. Let us visit his lady, who is dressing. Will she receive visitors? It depends; is that a hair piece her dresser is skilfully arranging? The lady would certainly call her hair her own, since she has paid for it, but she likes it to be thought that she owes it only to nature. A maid is placed on guard outside the door. She turns us back, saying: "Madam has gone out", or "Madam has migraine." This last excuse was so fashionable that Ovid tells us maliciously that the so-called headache covered up a great deal of feminine deceit.

If a young beauty had a naturally fine head of hair, she would encourage visitors to come and watch it being dressed; she will want them to admire her white shoulders.

The *cosmetae* bring caskets, exquisite examples of which are exhibited in the Naples museum. One particularly beautifully engraved silver casket was found in Pompeii. The nine Muses with which it is decorated suggest that it was à bookcase designed for some particularly splendid manuscript. At last the lock was opened. It contained jars of cooking fat.

"Jewelry was the Pompeian lady's great extravagance... The matron's necklaces are priceless; she wore very long pendants from the ear, and exquisite bracelets...

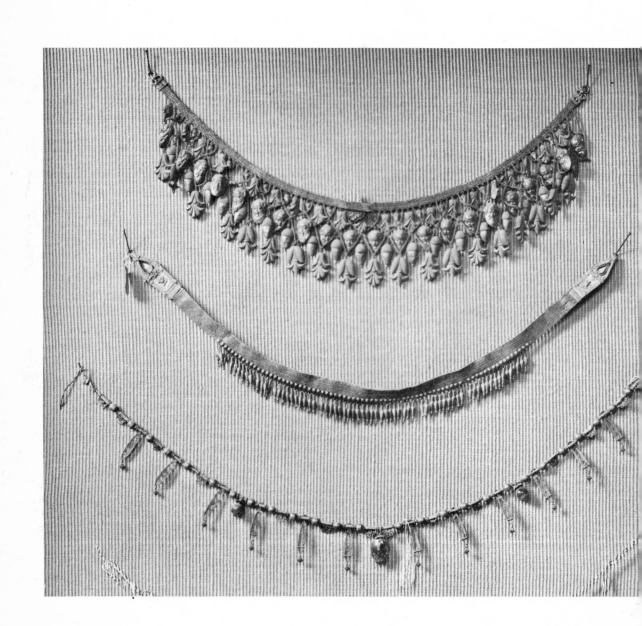

The soaps and cosmetics of every kind which have been preserved by Vesuvius certainly bear out the poets who vaunted the perfection of perfumery in the ancient world.

The dressing ceremony was so important for Roman matrons that Juvenal compares their boudoir to the terrible tribunal of Dionysius the Tyrant, which offered the choice only of honour or death. It was no good telling women that the fairest face is that given us by nature, without adornment—art was always called in to make it even more beautiful.

We have described the tribulations of the *ornatrix*. She needed skill and patience to please her mistress, who followed her smallest movement in the mirror. Strangely, although glass of every kind has been found in Pompeii, the mirrors were made of metal. Some were large enough for the lady to be able to see herself from head to foot. Mirrors from Brundusium were sold at amazing prices.

Long pins, which have been found in quantities, were used to curl and dress the hair. Care of the eyes and eyebrows followed attention to the hair. A malicious poet says to a woman: "Why do you provoke me with an eyebrow that was pencilled for you this morning?" But how much effort went into making up a face! There were fashionable complexions; it was modish to be a little pale.

The choice of the day's dress each morning: white was worn by brunettes and black by blondes; Briseis, when she was carried off, wore a white dress. Ovid tells us all these

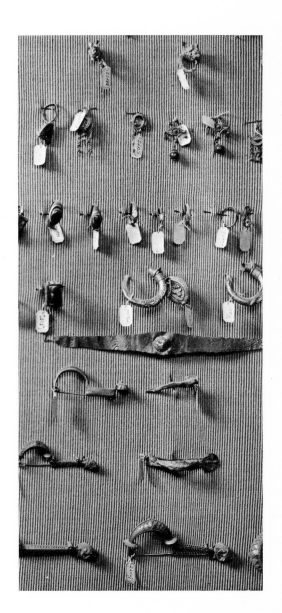

In the doctor's surgery a large quantity of instruments have been discovered which had been believed to be modern inventions; they had been highly developed in Pompeii. Some of these instruments are exhibited in the Naples museum (below).

things; but fashion had also discovered many other colours, and fashion always demands something new. Which one to choose; the blue of a cloudless sky, the green of the sea nymph, or the rose of dawn? The ashes of Pompeii have preserved impressions of various materials, and we can easily recognise their quality. There were cloths so fine that Petronius called them woven wind.

Jewelry was the Pompeian lady's great extravagance. Examples which have been recovered take up whole rooms in the museum. The matron would deck herself out with jewels from first thing in the morning. The diamond was not her favourite stone— the secret of cutting it was not yet known. The lady preferred fine pearls from the East. Her necklaces are priceless; her earrings exquisite. It is still fashionable to wear long pendants from the ear, despite Juvenal's protest against the folly of women who distended their ear-lobes in this way.

The bracelets were often exquisitely elegant, and Ovid can find no other fault in them than that they were too ornate. He tells us that he had seen one in the shape of a serpent in solid gold weighing as much as ten pounds. Rings were set with the finest and most beautifully cut stones. Pompeian ladies used to complain that they did not have enough fingers on which to wear them.

As we look at this enormous collection of cameos and gems, we recall Ovid's reproach to women on their extravagance. He asked them: "Why are you so anxious to carry your wealth on your person?" And Propertius: "Here comes a matron dressed in her descendants' inheritance!"

Once the lady had dressed herself in her finery, she needed to be seen wearing it. She leaves the town in a litter carried by Cappadocians. To attract the notice of the crowd the litter is preceded by black runners, shouting "Make way! Make way!"

Night falls; the evening is a time for pleasure. The covers on the couches are prepared. Before we go into the dining room, let us take a look at the kitchen.

To avoid the danger of fire and the nuisance of smoke and fumes, the kitchen was some distance from the dining room. Its annexes were the *horreum,* which stored winter provisions, the *olearium,* where oil was kept, and the *cellae vinariae,* where the wine was left to age. The Pompeians generally had several dining rooms; they lived very well. A room in the museum which attracts a great deal of interest is the one which exhibits the fruit, grain and remains of fish and game discovered under the table of a priest or rich man overcome by the eruption as he was eating. A dish contains a chicken casserole, the cooking of which was interrupted by the volcano.

What a variety of cooking utensils! Here is a stove designed to roast meat and heat water at the same time. Here is a pan with silver insets, here the pot-au-feu, the scoop, the tripod stand, the frying pan, the dripping pan, the scrubbing brush, and a considerable variety of kitchen moulds. The moulds come

"The Pompeians had several dining rooms..."—Banqueting scene (fresco) and photograph of the kitchen of the villa of the Mysteries.

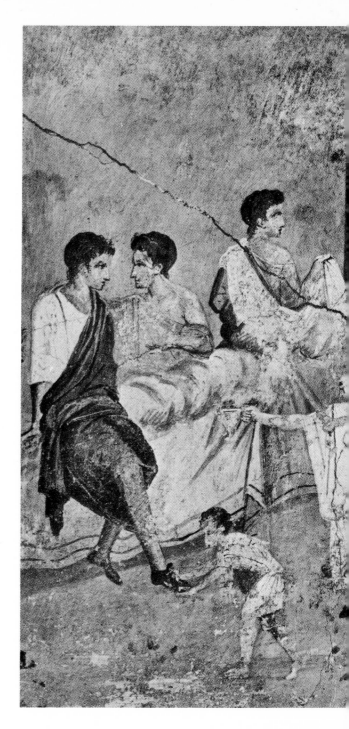

in charming shapes, and depict a hare, a sucking pig, a chicken spreading its wings.

The Roman god who was guardian of the kitchen was Fornax. In Pompeii he had more worshippers than did Mars.

Before entering the *triclinium,* or dining room, the Pompeians took care to dress in dinner clothes or *caenatoria vestis;* these were white or gaily coloured robes. They left their shoes outside, and wore elegant slippers.

According to custom, only three couches were set around the table; each couch could accommodate three people. Generally, there should be at table neither less than the three Graces nor more than the nine Muses. The couches were decorated with ivory, bronze and mother of pearl; they were set on raised pedestals.

It would have been a bad augury to cross the threshold of the dining room with the left foot. A slave was consequently stationed at the door to warn each guest, repeating the words: "Right foot."

The decoration of the table and the couches was magnificent. What remains tells us a great deal about Pompeian luxury: the elegance of the candelabra and the gold lamps which used to light the evening meals is striking.

The dazzle of the candles and the clouds of perfume falling from the ceiling joined with the bouquet of the wines and the taste of the most delicious dishes in an exquisite symphony which excited the imagination and flattered the senses.

Each guest brought his own tooth-pick, which he used discreetly, and a napkin, which he flaunted. He would be careful to take it away with him, unless he was lordly enough to leave it behind for the slaves who had served him.

The magnificence of the dinners of antiquity is indescribable. Never has human gluttony reached a higher peak than in the age of Lucullus and his numerous imitators. The masters of the Earth spared no expense to satisfy their most sensual appetites. The care they took over the feeding of their eels is well known. Crassus found it entirely appropriate to interrupt the Senate proceedings to lament the death of one of his eels. He loved it like a child, and went into mourning for it. The Pompeians, who engaged in trade with distant lands, brought tribute from afar to their table. They sought to buy from the best stocked oyster-beds, the largest fish-grounds, the richest aviaries, with shell-fish from Africa, birds from Phase, and gilded fruits from Italy and Sicily.

The art of cooking reached an unequalled perfection. Game was served in the form of a fish; enormous fish were served in the most surprising shapes. Live birds escaped from the side of a roast sucking-pig; nightingales' tongues were one of the most extravagant dishes. Pompeii was famous for its goose liver pâtés. The mushrooms were almost finer than truffles; though that, of course, was all a question of taste. Excellent olives, sardines, eggs seasoned with chopped anchovies were served as hors d'œuvres. Water-ices and ice-cream *(sorpata et gelata)* were already celebrated—a fame which Neapolitan ices continue to this day. Apicius wrote about the science of cooking. How careful the cook had to be! If he was unfortunate enough to serve a badly cooked hare or a spoiled sauce, he would be called out before the guests and soundly beaten.

The Pompeians liked good wine; they knew how to make it, care for it, and drink it. They labelled the amphoras, and noted the consulate under which the wine had been harvested; this was how the vintage was recorded. Falernian wine from the time of the Consul Opimius, aged 100 years, was particularly esteemed: *Falernum opinanum centum annorum.*

Acceptable behaviour amongst high society in Pompeii differed from that of our own age.

In the house of Menander: hearth where meat was grilled, and chest where a cache of table silver was discovered.

Below: Small table in the dining room of
the house of Menander.

Opposite: Still life "the partridge" (fresco
from a dining room).

Following pages: Vase for libations, and
fountain in a square.

"The splendour and elegance of the candelabras and lamps which brightly lit the evening meals tell us a great deal about the extravagance of Pompeian life."

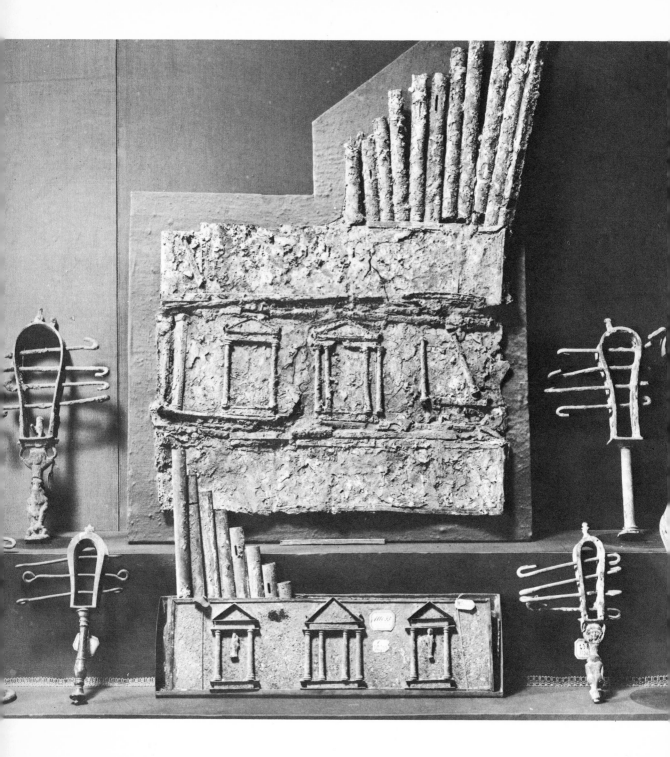

It was quite well considered for wealthy Pompeians to drink until they were intoxicated. "I see no harm", Tibullus writes, "in steeping oneself in wine on feast days." Wine was considered the strongest antidote to hemlock. To be forced by fear of death to drink to the greatest excess, a Pompeian would sometimes deliberately poison himself with hemlock—which takes drunkenness to heroic lengths. It was the best form to feign drunkenness without losing rationality, to be able to say whatever one wanted, letting the excellence of the wine and the abundance of the drink excuse any indiscretion.

Extravagant language was common. "A witticism likely to be remembered is one that burns the mouth", says Cicero. The Pompeians enjoyed slightly improper jokes and even obscenities. Freedom in language was permitted socially, and in poetry, and there was nothing incompatible with the strictest standards in personal life. "My muse is licen-

Left: Musical instruments in bronze from the early Pompeian period. Right: Vessel designed to keep water cool.

tious, but my life is not", Martial writes. And Catullus says: "A poet should be personally chaste, but there is no reason why his poetry should be!" If a Pompeian girl blushed she would be reminded of these lines from Ovid, the fashionable poet: "You blushed! The flush suits your pale complexion, but it is useful only if it is feigned. Otherwise, it can only harm you."

When the jokes became too broad, the girls, instead of leaving the table, would try to provoke the conversation further. Ovid considered that it was not good form for a woman to over-eat, but he saw nothing wrong in her drinking a little too much.

The girls' especial task was to encourage the guests to drink, cajoling them with whispered entreaties. Who could refuse to empty the cup as many times as the lady had letters in her name?

Finally, when the loving cup, in which the master mixed rose petals with the sweetest

Right: Rustic table.

68

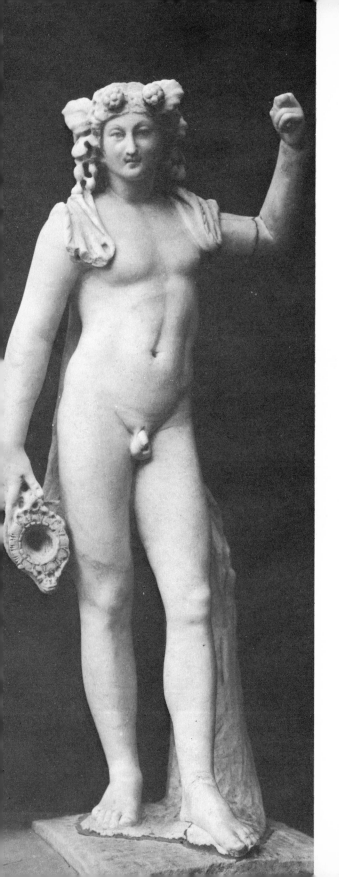

nectar, had circulated a last time, it was time for music. The Pompeian girls, who knew that the beauty of the voice could charm as much as the beauty of the face, learned early to sing. Others would play the harp, the cithera or the lyre.

The Pompeians did not dance with each other as we do. They liked to be entertained by paid dancing girls. How beautiful they were! How agile and graceful! How well did the clothes floating over their superb bodies excite desire by what they revealed and what they concealed! The paintings of the period allow us to see the voluptuous scenes which adorned the feasts of antiquity.

But the excitement of wine, beauty and music was not enough to satisfy jaded palates. More vivid emotions were needed. Blood was required to end off the evening. Here are the gladiators, men whose job is to

"Acceptable behaviour amongst high society in Pompeii differed from that of our own age. It was quite well consider-ed for wealthy Pompeians to drink until they were intoxicated. It was the best form to feign drunkenness without losing rationality..." Opposite: Marble statuette of Bacchus from the house of the Vettii.

The Pompeian brothel was famous: this is the entrance, through which couples reached the first floor directly.

kill each other for money. They are strong and proud, full of life and youth; they have come to die a graceful death. They fight with murderous zeal and fierce energy. What a fine sight to watch the skill with which they take such terrible blows! The guests' pleasure reaches its peak when the combatants, covered in wounds, fall beneath the table, mixing their blood with wine from the upturned cups!

4. Life outside the home

Pompeii was not a place where the cult of hearth and home flourished. Most of a citizen's life was spent away from his doors.

The *forum romanum* played an immensely important part in the history of the ancient world; the Pompeian forum still retains the monuments which attest to its significance.

Each town wanted to have a forum on the Roman model. According to Varro, the word derives from *ferrendo;* it was the main square to which goods were brought to be sold, law suits to be judged, and matters of local importance to be discussed. The number of fora varied according to the size of the town. It became very large when the Rome of Augustus wanted to show through its magnificence that it was worthy to be the capital of the universe.

Apart from the famous forum at the foot of the Capitoline Hill there was also the *forum boarium,* cattle market; the *forum piscarium,* fish market, the *forum pistorium,* bread market; the *forum cupendinis,* luxury food market, and many others. It would take too long to list them all.

There were several places in Pompeii where markets were held every nine days; we shall only discuss the civil forum, where popular assemblies were held. The forum was a meeting point. Seven roads led to it. Around about are the ruins of fine buildings and beautiful temples; it is one of the most important sites in the town.

The forum, based on the Greek *agora,* was in the shape of an elongated parallelo-

gram, 518 feet long and 106 feet wide. It was paved in white travertine stone, and surrounded by elegant Doric columns which supported a two-storey portico. On every side were full length statues of famous men, erected at the town's expense during their lifetimes or immediately following their deaths; 22 fine marble pedestals, most of them unfinished, still stand. The forum also included four equestrian statues and a *quadriga,* a magnificent triumphal arch facing the sea, and a splendid temple.

Statues were set all along the top of the porticos, which led to terraces reached by staircases outside the forum. Perhaps this arrangement was intended to allow ladies to reach the galleries without having to pass through the crowds in the forum. Or perhaps it made it easier for the wealthy citizen to take up a good position on important occasions before the iron gates sealing off the forum were opened to the public.

The civil forum was in the process of being rebuilt when the eruption suddenly interrupted the work. No special archaeological knowledge is needed to distinguish between the parts of the forum which were already in ruins and those which had not been completed. Artistic decadence was already evident, and it is striking in the comparison between the old and the recently finished column capitals. Even at this distant time, architects knew very well how to spoil old buildings on the pretext of restoring and embellishing them.

Following Vitruvius's advice, the forum was

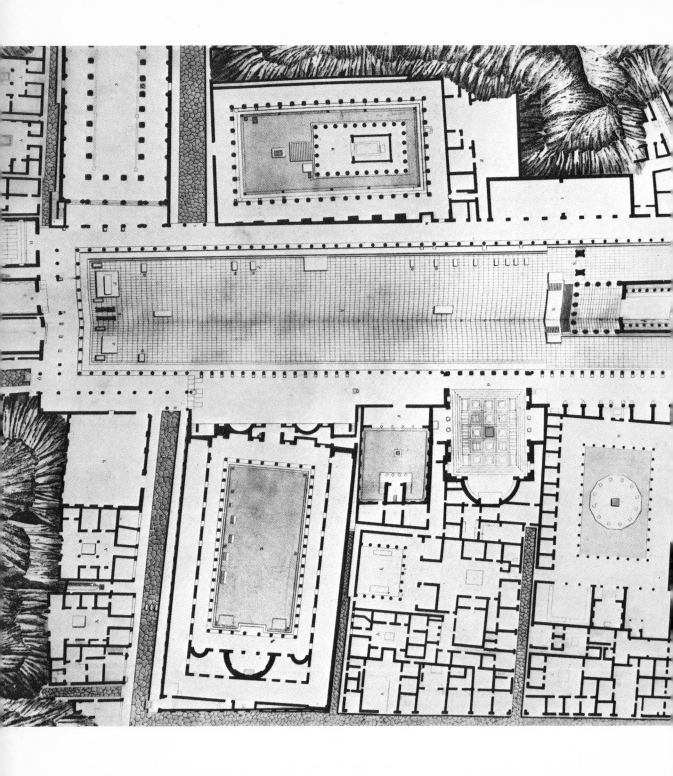

"The forum also included four equestrian statues and a quadriga, a magnificent triumphal arch and a splendid temple."—Ground plan of the forum.

built close to the sea. It was here that the Pompeian spent the greater part of his day while the slaves worked in his house. He would discuss the latest news, and seated on the shore, would look out to sea, searching the horizon for a white sail, perhaps a boat returning from Egypt or more distant lands.

Often, steeped in revery, he would spend careless hours in contemplation of the waves, whose blue rivalled that of the skies. This was the place where lovers met. Ovid recommended that the man should arrive early, as ladies should not be kept waiting.

Town politics were also discussed in the forum.

A glance at the customs house or weights and measures inspectorate is enough to tell us that markets were held here. Scales and weights of all sorts and sizes have been found in this office. In the distant past the market and court cases were held on the same spot. Later, justice was dispensed in special buildings called *basilicae*. The one in Pompeii was at the same time a courthouse and an exchange.

The building was open to the sky, with its nave lined by graceful Ionic columns. The coupled columns at the angles remind us of Gothic churches.

At the end of the hall sat the judges on their raised seats. Beneath their feet were the dungeons, which were reached by small, narrow stairways. The accused knew he had been convicted when the trap-door was raised.

Vaulted, lightless cellars have been found near the forum; these must have been the prisons. Skeletons have been discovered here with irons attached to their feet. But we shall not discuss the rigours of punishment in antiquity. In the barracks four skeletons were discovered attached to an iron bar, which had bolts and pins allowing the prisoner to lie down even though his legs were in chains.

The northern edge of the forum consisted of a temple where a huge bust of Jupiter has been found.

Around the base of the temple were twelve shops, which did not have access to it. One of the shops contained glass jars and a hundred and fifty little bottles. In others were quantities of fruit, art objects and a variety of merchandise.

Meetings in the temple were not always religious occasions, and the Pompeians did not believe they were profaning consecrated ground by carrying out all sorts of business there. The flight of steps leading to the temple of Jupiter was used as a tribune by orators who harangued the crowd gathered in the forum.

The early Roman religion was a confusion of diverse Italic beliefs, and it was supplanted by the Greek faith. Jupiter, master of the world but still subject to destiny and all human weaknesses, had his temple in Pompeii, but the deities which seem to have attracted the greatest number of worshippers in this town of pleasure and money were Mercury,

Fortuna, Venus and Isis.

The temple of Mercury was in the forum. This was the appropriate spot recommended by Vitruvius for the god of trade. No building in the town had a more irregular shape; it was a sort of lozenge. The interior was small. The altar is remarkable for its sculptures, which represent a sacrifice and tell the instruments used in religious ceremonies.

In its early days Rome had very little sea trade. She did not therefore include a god of trade amongst her national deities. Later she filled this gap by adopting the Greek god Hermes, whom she named Mercury— *a mercurium cura.* Pompeii was one of the towns most dependent on trade in all the Mediterranean basin. Mercury had a special right to the Pompeians' homage; he protected their distant ships, and encouraged the making of easy fortunes. By sprinkling his idol with a laurel branch dipped in water and offering a few prayers to the god, the merchant hoped he would spare his business the consequences of frauds committed and about to be committed.

The patron of traders was also the guardian of thieves. He stole himself, and he had a hard task to look after those who tried to imitate him. He did a variety of jobs, including some which were not particularly impressive; he was, for instance, Jupiter's messenger.

The temple of Fortuna was built on a back street. Four steps lead up to the altar, and another nine go to the rounded sanctuary in the middle of which, on a pedestal, was an idol of the goddess. Other statues were set in four niches.

The oldest and largest temple in Pompeii was dedicated to the patron goddess of the town, *Venus physica pompeiana.*

As we have seen, monuments which had suffered in the previous eruption were in the process of being rebuilt, with more extravagance than taste. The temple of Venus was, indeed, unfinished. In the middle of a huge courtyard and faced by an eighteen-column portico, it was 66 feet long, 121 feet wide and 10 feet high. The interior is decorated with fine murals. The painter shows beautiful landscapes, grotesque figures and Homeric scenes. The altar is white marble. Two really beautiful statues represent Venus and a Faun.

Venus felix, symbol of female fertility, was especially worshipped in Campania; several temples dedicated to her have been found in this beautiful land, where everything seems to be an invitation to enjoyment. The worship of the *Venus physica* of Pompeii was perhaps part of this tradition.

The Egyptian cult of Isis was also practised in Pompeii. Her temple is truly remarkable. It is reached by a flight of ten steps. The sanctuary is decorated by fine Doric columns with red and white shafts. Everything in the temple reminds the worshipper of Egypt; the candelabra are in lotus shapes; the sistrum is represented on every side. At the doorway was a collecting box, and two basins for the lustral water; there are vases for water sacred to the Egyptian deities.

It was the custom to share the sacrificial

Opposite: A view of the forum. Below:
Remains of the temple of Apollo.

Following pages: Symbols from the altar
in the temple of Augustus.—The Marine
gate.

The fountain of Mercury ("The god who was the patron of merchants was also the guardian of thieves").
Below: Fresco depicting the twelve gods of Olympus, discovered behind the fountain at a point where processions halted and sacrifices were made.

offerings with the gods. All ceremonies, whether public or private, were consequently followed by a feast. The priests of Isis were at table when the volcano overcame them; martyrs to their gluttony, they preferred to die rather than abandon their dinner. The menu of their last meal has been preserved in the ash.

In the temple we find representations of Isis, sistrum in hand, Anubis with the dog's head, Venus in marble, Bacchus, Priapus and cupids and nymphs at play. Isis was not renowned for her morality; she was known as the corruptress. When Ovid wrote of the art of love he was careful to ask: "Why should you flee the temple of the cow of Memphis, this Isis who allowed herself to be seduced and who recruits so many women to follow her example?"

One can believe all the excesses that are recorded about the worship of Isis when one sees in Pompeii the Roman gods who accompanied the foreign deity. At her side were Venus, goddess of love, Priapus and Bacchus, god of wine. Ovid might have been thinking particularly of this region when he wrote that wine produced an outpouring of emotion and warm passions.

The worship of Isis, which the old Romans disapproved, well suited the inhabitants of Pompeii. We shall say no more of the festivals instituted in honour of the Egyptian goddess. But what of the secrets of the initiations into the mysteries of Isis? Apuleius replies: "No doubt, studious reader,

your curiosity will be aroused by what is said and done at these initiation ceremonies. I would tell you if I were allowed to tell; you would learn if you were allowed to learn. But the crime would be equal for ear and tongue in complicity with this reckless curiosity."

We should recall that the worst of the Roman emperors were the most devoted followers of Isis and the most assiduous attenders at her orgies.

"The worship of Isis well suited the inhabitants of Pompeii... The crime would be equal for ear and tongue if we were to describe the secrets of the initiations into the mysteries of Isis."—Cross-section of the temple of Isis by Piranesi. Pompeian painting depicting religious ceremony in honour of the goddess.

Inscription on a tomb in front of the gate of Vesuvius.

5 - Graffiti

Pliny, Lucian and St Jerome tell us of the Romans' habit of writing or engraving their thoughts on walls and columns. They were sometimes epigrammatic, and sometimes erotic. This custom was widely adopted by the Pompeians.

In houses, walls prepared for murals were also available for ingenious or pithy comments. The soldier amused himself by scribbling the graffiti found in the barracks; the litigant and the idler, who spent their time in the law court, got rid of some of their spite or boredom in the remarks with which they covered the walls of the basilica.

On the streets our advertising hoardings found their counterparts in the *alba*, panels which were designed for official announcements or private advertisements, which appeared in black or red characters. These *alba* were decorated with pilasters and divided into a number of sections; one had no less than 23 divisions.

The Pompeians enjoyed reading graffiti, and they wrote them everywhere. When they passed the door of someone they admired, they would write a few compliments or good wishes on his wall. "Terentius Euxodus is a fine man", one tells us, "he supports his friends and defends them in every way." Or again: "Great success to Terentius, *Terentio feliciter*." Another is more gallant, and no doubt met with the approval of the lady of the house. The writer could not resist the temptation to address a respectful greeting: "Gemelus to Caserna, wife of L. Mumisius, hail!"

Inscriptions were made in charcoal, brush, stylet, chisel, mosaic.

We have already mentioned the welcomes inscribed on the doorstep at the entrance to houses. A mosaic reads "*Salve, lucru,* hail, wealth!" Traders wrote on their weights and measures: "*Eme, et habebis,* buy and you shall have." On a charming lamp decorated with a face and a flower, someone has wished himself a happy new year: "*Annum novum faustum mihi.*"

The people of Pompeii spoke three languages: Oscan, Greek and Samnite. They spoke Latin badly, and they wrote as they spoke. They spelt words according to their own pronunciation. Thus you can find the beginning of the Aeneid written: "*Alma vilumque cano*" instead of "*arma virumque cano*"; and "*abiat iradum*" for "*habeat iratum*".

A dispute which had considerable consequence arose between the people of Pompeii and those of Nuceria. On one feast day in Pompeii, a gladiatorial combat attracted crowds from all the surrounding regions to the amphitheatre. A few heated words led to a dispute which ended in bloody conflict. The more numerous Pompeians massacred the visitors. The Nucerians brought an action against the Pompeians, and judgment was returned in their favour. The Pompeian ring-leaders were arrested and exiled, and the population as a whole was deprived of the theatre for a period of ten years. Beneath a scrawled caricature one can read the inscription: "Campanians, in your victory you have suffered as great a defeat as the Nucerians! *Campani, victoria una cum Nucerinis periistis.*"

The inscriptions engraved on marble tables or the pedestals of statues have told us a great deal about the use and ownership of buildings and monuments. We learn from them names and organization of the city administration, and the buildings that its members erected. In the forum, for example, an inscriptions tells us that "V. Papidius, son of Epidius, Quaestor, built these porticos."

Pompeii had a great many sundials. Those near the temples were often surrounded by semi-circular benches. "L. Sepunius Sandilanus and Lucius M. Herenius, *Duoviri* responsible for the administration of justice, have erected a bench and a sundial at their own expense."

The epitaphs carved in the stone of the tombs did not ask for prayers for the departed, as is the Christian custom. They were intended only to flatter vanity or excite curiosity.

Propertius preferred anonymity to such sterile praise. "After my death," he wrote, "I should not care to have my name ever-lastingly displayed on the public highway."

But smaller minds in Pompeii felt it was most important to leave posterity with a fine impression of the honours they had received. They do not fail to let it be known that they were *Aediles, Duoviri, Quaestores,*

that they had received the honour of the *bisellium,* and above all that the town had granted them free of charge a large plot of land on which to build their tomb.

The style of the epitaphs shows no brilliant variety. This example is representative:

"To Marcus Alleius Lucius, *Libella,* first *Aedile, Duumvir,* Quinquennial *Praefectus,* and to Marcus Alleius his son, *Decurio* who died aged seventeen, the people has given the land on which this tomb is built. Alleia Decimilla, public priestess of Ceres, has erected this monument to her husband and their son."

The finest tombs were not always built by legitimate wives. One ruined vault bears the inscription: "Servilia to the love of her heart."

Advertisements displayed on street corners were expected to be treated with respect; anyone who defaced them was subject to the anger of Venus. Notices covered a great many subjects. There are offers of rewards for the return of an object that had been lost or stolen; advertisements by tradesmen and inn-keepers: "Traveller, if you go from here to the twelfth tower, you will find Sarinus, son of Pubius, who owns an inn. Greetings." This inscription, like many of those intended to be read by the common people, was written in Oscan script. There are several notices advertising lodging houses.

"Sittius has reopened the Elephant boarding house, *triclinium* with three couches, all comforts." "In the Arriana Polliana

insula, owned by Alifius Nigidius major, shops with cenacles and climbing vines are offered for rent from the first of the Ides of July." Climbing vines were the ornament of the terrace; the cenacle was on the mezzanine floor. Plutarch tells us that Sylla spent his childhood on the mezzanine floor.

"To let on the estate of Julia Felix, Daughter of Spurius, from 1st to 6th Ides of August, a venereum and 90 shops. S.Q.D. L.E.N.C." There have been several interpretations of these letters. One expert believes that it simply means that the lease could be renewed by tacit consent: *Si quinquennium decurrunt, locatio erit mudo conr. sensu:* after five years the lease will continue by mutual agreement.

As in our own time, electoral posters appeared on the walls. They tended to be

Wall drawing. Epitaph from a tomb: *"These epitaphs did not ask for prayers for the departed. They were intended to excite curiosity."*

"As in our own time, electoral posters appeared on the walls. But instead of recommending himself, the candidate had himself promoted by his friends... A large number of theatre posters have also been discovered." Above: Election notices and theatre posters on a wall in the Street of the Amphitheatre. Right: An unknown.

the slave wanted to say.

The harder the master, the more he needed to be flattered. The man who least deserved praise received the most. But a powerful man could sometimes be irritated by such insincerities. Thus one of Plautus's characters remarks caustically: "I feel no need to have my walls covered with scribbled eulogies."

A great many of the inscriptions were congratulations to those who entertained the people in gladiatorial bouts, at the theatre or on feast days. Compliments were generally inspired by scarcely veiled personal interest. Insults derived from common envy and malice. Some epigrams were particularly biting; the walls of the basilica were covered with examples.

The dissatisfied litigant did not spare the judge; he could find an outlet for his anger in safe anonymity. Cicero tells us that above the tribunal, actually inscribed on a bust of Verres, were many complaints about Pipa, his mistress. "*Quid pretium legi?—*What price justice?" This reminds us of Propertius's lines: "Gold can do anything; gold can overcome trust, right and justice." One man threatens his neighbour with litigation; another condemns a woman for going to court. Sometimes an insult is brutal: "Barca, you deserve to die!"

Some epigrams had style and wit: "Suavis, the wine merchant's wife is thirsty; I pray that she is thirsty enough to drink all her own wine." Some inscriptions are full-length satires. Rufus is condemned for his arrogance and love of pomp. He is compared with Vibius, a very rich and distinguished man, who has never been seen strolling on Portunus square with a cane in his hand, something that Rufus does every day.

The Pompeians' sensuality is of course also revealed in their graffiti. As are their flights of passion: "Augea loves Arabienus"— "Farewell. Try to love me. *Vale. Fac me ames*"—"Only he who loves is happy."— "I should rather die than be a god without you!"—"I love a blonde, and now all brunettes disgust me." Another hand has added underneath this line: "You hate brunettes, but despite yourself you will return to them. I tell you so. Signed, Venus Physica of Pompeii."

Public foutain on he Street of Plenty beside a wall depicting the twelve gods of Olympus (see page 85).

M. Vecilio Verecondo: tradesman's sign on the Street of Plenty.

Left: Statue of Jupiter.

Right: "Maenad": fresco from Pompeii, now in the Naples museum.

Following pages: Bust of Diana and pastoral scene—bronze and fresco from Pompeii.

The theatre; a Roman woman from the time of Pompeii.

"The uncovering of Pompeii revealed treasures which were believed lost for ever."—Reconstruction of a room in the house of the Vettii.

6 – The murals

Greek architecture is known to us through the marvellous monuments which have survived the centuries; it is enough to see them to admire them. The Romans had to admit the superiority of Greek art; they carried off the finest examples as booty, and the masters of the Earth brought the greatest foreign artists to their own country.

We know the names of the great painters of antiquity, but most of their work has disappeared. Descriptions of some of their paintings remain, and we know how highly prized they could be. Mummius, responsible for the sale of plunder from Corinth, refused 100 talents for a *Bacchus*. Conquered towns could pay off ransoms with a picture. Demetrius Poliocretes gave up a siege of Rhodes in order to avoid Protogenes, who had his studio in the one spot from which the town could be taken.

The uncovering of Pompeii revealed treasures which were believed lost for ever. The walls of the houses of private individuals, as well as those of the temples of the gods, were covered in the most brilliant murals. The discovery of a paintmaker's workshop teaches us that colours were fixed in resin; it had erroneously been believed that the encaustic process had been used.

Three-quarters of the themes chosen by the artists were mythological subjects. The painter worked to the order of the citizen who commissioned him to decorate his house, and he had to accommodate himself to every taste and paint in all styles. One would want portraits, another landscapes. The artist would pass from the real to the ideal, from scenes of pure imagination to scenes of Pompeiian daily life, from original work to reproductions of masterpieces, as the fancy took his patron.

The landscapes show faults in perspective. They are not highly finished, but they are skilfully executed; the arabesques reach a matchless perfection, and the great tableaux were clearly painted by Greek artists.

Composition is exquisitely delicate. Nudes, faces and folds in clothing are as graceful as one would expect in the ancient world. The clothing is so light that it allows a glimpse of the gentle curves of the body beneath. The feel and sureness of the draughtmanship is admirable.

A particularly fine black and white sketch shows five girls playing dibs with little counters which they have added to the game to make it more interesting. Their names are written by their sides: Latone, Niobe, Phoebe, Hiboera and Aglaë. These are well known names, but we do not know who the gamesplayers were. At the base of the picture are the words: painted by Alexander of Athens.

To preserve the precious frescos, which would deteriorate rapidly in roofless houses exposed to the elements, it was decided to remove them from the walls and store them in the museum, where they are properly classified.

Indeed, Pliny tells us that when the old

temple of Ceres in Rome was being repaired the murals were removed and framed. He also tells us: "Murena and Varro, when they were *Aediles,* removed a fine mural painted on brick in Lacedaemon, and had it taken to Rome, where it was framed and hung in the Comitia."

The sujects which seemed to be the most appreciated were those which could least be said to have a high moral content. The artist thus delights in reproducing the loves of Venus and Mars. Here a cupid disarms the hero, and another offers scents to the goddess of beauty. Here, so as not to be surprised. the lovers are guarded by a watchdog.

The worship of Bacchus was particularly honoured in Pompeii. Vesuvian wines were highly thought of; the Pompeians thought nothing better than to fortify themselves within with good wine, while coating their bodies with oil. Wine was not merely a health-giving drink; its effects produced drunken scenes at the so-called religious festivals—which would shock a great many people today.

How many fine paintings did Bacchus inspire! Here he is discovering the abandoned Ariadne; here a faun surprises a sleeping Bacchante. In this picture the Bacchantes are wearing strange symbols—look at that beautiful girl whose hair is prettily curled with vine leaves and grapes!

If Pompeian paintings shed a new light on the history of art in antiquity, they also tell us a great deal about the details of everyday life. They complete information that was missing; they serve as a commentary on the graffiti.

From the murals we have a very clear idea of what the furniture destroyed by the volcano looked like. We rediscover how the doors were made—as well as other articles that have disappeared.

In the house of Marcus Lucretius is a painting which shows all the instruments used in writing: the wax-covered tablet; the stylet; the writing stand; the reeds; the seal. And that is not all. The address is already on the letter: *M. Lucretio Flam. Martis, decurioni Pompeii*—to Marcus Lucretius, *Flamen* of Mars, *Decurio* of Pompeii.

The murals are particularly informative about the Roman games, which were a Pompeian passion. They are depicted everywhere, in marble bas-reliefs, in paintings by the great artists; in graffiti scrawled on roadside walls. Thanks to the artist's brush, we also know exactly what happened during religious ceremonies. Look at this painting of a sacrifice; priests in long robes pour incense from their *paterae;* then they sacrifice their offerings while choirs of boys and girls sing *Venus genitrix.*

It would be instructive to make a study of Roman music from the wall paintings of Pompeii. In Sallust's house an old faun is shown teaching a young man to play the seven-fluted hornpipe; examples of several of the instruments have been found; others we

Contemporary paintings show what were doubtless leading citizens and matrons seated in a sort of bar, their heads enveloped in hoods to avoid recognition.

Invitations to drink are frequently shown on inn-signs. After drinking, it was time to gamble. Murals and inscriptions tell us about the games that were played. Those which required skill were less favoured than games which excited greed. How great were the sums lost at dibs, chess and dice!

The Romans called chess *latrunculi*. They used a chessboard on which the different pieces represented bandit gangs disputing possession of a strong-point.

The great gamblers preferred to play dice. They used a dice-box. Roman dice were very like ours, with the same arrangement of spots. All sixes was the throw of Venus; all aces, the throw of the dog.

The passion for gambling was one of the great vices of antiquity. Women were as caught up as men. They were careful to conceal their disappointment at losing; for as Ovid rightly says, nothing blemished beauty more than not knowing how to hide frustration. It was considered good form to allow oneself to be beaten when playing with women—particularly, no doubt, when they were pretty and the stakes small.

Ovid tells us about a handsome young man who joins a gambling school. His hair is perfumed. He wears an elegant belt. He pays court to the ladies. Be careful, ladies, what he is saying to you he has said to many others before you.—He sighs... The thief! His sighs are not for your hearts, but your wallets! To begin with he loses, he loses with style, he loses a lot, but soon he has won even more. His loaded dice assure him of a massive profit. He does not know when to stop; he has won too much, and it is that which ruins him. His fraud is discovered. The players become abusive; there are struggles, scuffles, shouts of rage and regret. Anger shows on all the faces; insults give way to blows. The table is toppled, and lies there upside down.

The Pompeians enjoyed gambling; their great passion was the Roman games. Games were held to forestall the vengeance of the gods or to obtain their favour. They were held after funerals, in honour of the dead. Games were held on a thousand occasions to win popular favour.

A pleasure which the sensual Romans, and like them the Pompeians, developed to a peak which we would find difficult to imagine, was the daily bath. This delightful and luxuriant custom was adopted by the Moslems; but it has never had a great deal of success with Christians.

There is no doubt that in antiquity the baths were a hygienic necessity under a burning sky at a time when the lack of good clothes and solid shoes made cleanliness more necessary than ever.

The baths were sumptuous palaces, magnificently decorated, where the Pompeians would spend their days dealing with impor-

"A pleasure which Pompeii developed to a peak which we would find difficult to imagine was the daily public bath." Palaestra of Stabia baths and brazier.

tant business or listening to idle gossip, engaging in political intrigues and love affairs, enjoying the delights of study and the joys of idleness, pampering their vanity and exhausting it with all the refinements of the pleasures of the senses excited by dance, music and other delights.

The Pompeian baths occupy almost an entire *insula*—a space 165 feet long and 175 feet deep. A corridor with a blue ceiling set with gold stars takes us from the *atrium* to the cloakroom. Three lines of benches still stand, as does the clothes counter. A sword has been left there. This small round room, lit from above, was where cold baths were taken; the *frigidarium*. Next comes the hot room or *tepidarium,* then the steam room or *caldarium.* And note the graceful columns, the stucco decorations, the murals, all remarkably well preserved.

The main brasier is in bronze; it stands on five feet, two of which are decorated with sphinxes. The basin is elegantly ornamented; we particularly notice a relief of a cow, *vacula,* and an inscription which tells us the name of the donor, M. Nigidius Vaccula. Several of the most aristocratic Roman families had taken their names from animals: Porcius, Taurus, Aper.

Nothing earned the gratitude of the populace more than funds dedicated to the embellishment of a place in which it took its pleasures. Thus Oscan and Latin inscriptions tell us which *Quaestor* set up the sundial from funds derived from court fines, and who paid for the building or rebuilding of the administrative office, the *destrictorium* (massage parlour), the portico or the *palaestra.*

Service at the baths was impeccable; opening time was signalled by the tolling of a bell. Entrance was not free of charge, but for the poor it was very cheap. "While, proud as a king, you go to the baths for only a quadrant", writes Horace. And several quadrants, low value coins, have indeed been found in a room in the Pompeian baths.

The wealthy had their own time—fairly late. For them the baths were relatively expensive. In the *spolarium,* where they undressed, they gave their clothes to *casparii,* who stored them in *caspae,* casks. They took what we would call Turkish baths, passing very quickly from extremely hot to very cold water. After sweating in the steam room, they were massaged by *tractores,* who scraped their skins with the strigil, a sort of curved metal or ivory comb. The rich man would have his slave bring his own elegant strigil, so as not to have to use the one provided by the establishment. After a skilful massage, the *reunctarii aliptae* shaved the customer and rubbed him with scents. The Romans must have had a particular passion for baths, for as Pliny tells us, they used to take as many as seven in the same day. A large part of the day and even the night was spent in the baths, which were lit in the evenings.

What were the pleasures which kept the Pompeians there so long? The baths did not

only offer physical enjoyments—there were also a centre for intellectual pleasures. After physical exercises and games, the customers liked to listen to lines from the poets. At this time, when all the elegance of life had reached such a degree of perfection, unhappy the man who spoke the language of Cicero and Virgil badly! Petronius tells us of one Eumolpius who, having tried to read some worthless verses, found it difficult to dodge the blows with which the people wanted to reward him.

Men and women bathed together in the town of Venus. Is was only fifty years after the destruction of Pompeii that the Emperor Hadrian, roused to indignation at the abuses that occurred, ordered the separation of the sexes and a return to ancient customs inspired by respect for morality.

The Pompeians loved lavish entertainment; they had an odeum and an amphitheatre. On the hillside overlooking the town was the great tragic theatre. In front of the theatre was a triangular forum, encircled by porticos made up of ninety Doric columns; the visitor was shaded from sun and rain.

The theatre was rebuilt after the eruption in 63 AD by the architect Artorius at the expense of Rufus and Halcorius, two wealthy citizens. It was not finished until 79 AD. It had seats for five thousand, and was ideally situated, open to gentle breezes from the sea.

In antiquity the theatre was not considered a profane but a noble place. Frequently, when important issues aroused public debate, the mob would insist that the judges leave their tribunal and adjourn to the theatre.

The Pompeian theatre was divided into the *postscenium,* backstage; the *scenium,* stage; the *proscenium,* stalls; the *orchestra,* pit—more precisely the area used for dances; the *caveae,* tiers where seats were numbered. The *vomitoria* where the exits; there were four outside and six inside the theatre.

There were 28 tiers, in Paros marble—several with seat numbers still visible. The first fourteen rows were the best seats. Roscia's law only permitted citizens with a fortune of at least 400,000 sesterces to use them. A curule-chair has been found in this area; the *bisellium* was brought into the auditorium. A railed-off gallery was especially reserved for women. The upper tiers, *summae caveae,* were used by slaves, by the mob, by men dressed in grey and working-class women. These theatre-goers were known as *pullati,* and in Italy the upper galleries are still called *piccionaja,* chicken hutch. *De summa cavea spectare,* to watch from the upper tier, became a proverbial expression to describe the mob.

Above the theatre, which was open to the sky, are cantilevers which supported the beams from which the *velarium* hung. It was in Campania that the custom of covering the auditorium with veils originated, so as to provide shade against the sun's rays. Like all good inventions, this one was at first hotly criticized, but in the end it triumphed over its critics. Some authors reproved the Ro-mans for imitating Asiatic flabbiness in allow-ing the plebeians to shelter in the shade.

The *velarium* was spread and folded by an ingenious mechanism. Suetonius tells us that it was one of Caligula's greatest amuse-ments to draw back the veils as soon as the audience had comfortably settled themselves in the shade. He enjoyed the irritation of the crowd, suddenly exposed to a burning sun.

Nero had a purple *velarium* fringed with gold and painted with scenes in which he was shown as Apollo drawing the sun's chariot. As shade was particularly valued under the burning sky of Italy, on important occasions the street were covered with veils hung be-tween the houses. Julius Caesar had shades set on the forum and along the sacred way, from his palace to the Capitol.

Advertisements for entertainments often promised shade: *vela erunt,* there will be veils.

Near the great tragic theatre was the odeum, or covered theatre. It only seated 1,500. The odeum was where comedies were played, where sceptres and crowns were awarded as prizes for poetry, and where plays were performed during the slack season—so as not to leave lewd pleasures idle during winter, as Tertullian puts it.

But it was the amphitheatre which was the principal place for public amusement. The one in Pompeii had twenty thousand seats; the Colosseum in Rome had more than a hundred thousand.

The amphitheatre was on the south-eastern

edge of the town. It was a combination of two theatres. The double pit—*orchestra*—was in the arena. Three main passageways opened onto it; one for gladiators, one for animals, the third for hands whose job it was to remove the corpses. Steps led to covered boxes, reserved for women.

Let us watch a performance. There is a long queue, and to relieve their boredom, people are writing their comments on the walls. They tell us about the exploits of the gladiators, and we learn, for example, that one of them had won fifty bouts.

There are seats reserved for slaves, but there are not enough of them for the numbers who covet them, and they go to those who have been up early to queue for them. Important people, or those who already have tickets, are taken to their seats by ushers.

The most lavish entertainments are staged in the amphitheatre. The easiest way to please the people and the act of generosity which was rewarded with the greatest glory was the holding of a gladiatorial combat. Wealthy citizens commonly left a legacy for the holding of an annual combat to celebrate the anniversary of their deaths.

The mania for giving performances became so contagious that poorer citizens tried to emulate the rich; this was a good way of honouring a father's memory and enhancing popularity. To prevent people ruining themselves, a *Senatus consultum* forbad those whose income was less than 400,000 sesterces from organizing gladiatorial bouts. Wiser

citizens who were obliged to make similar donations to the municipality often preferred to give the enormous sums that others wasted on a single day's entertainment for some more permanent memorial, as is evidenced by several inscriptions.

The notices advertised the kind of combat that was to be organized: *venatio,* the hunt, and *munera,* or hand-to-hand bouts between gladiators. There were several sorts of hunt. Sometimes animals were set against each other; sometimes they were made to fight men. A poster tells us that the show will start at sunrise. We learn from Suetonius that Claudius so enjoyed these spectacles that he would go to the circus at daybreak and stay until dinner time.

During Trajan's reign, at the games held to commemorate the defeat of the Parthians, 11,000 animals were killed in the arena.

Murals at the Pompeian amphitheatre tell us what happened there. A horse flees from a lion; a tiger fights a boar; a bear is roped together with a bull. The sculptures on tombs also tell us about the hunts. A bas-relief on Codrus's crypt depicts all sorts of animals: lions, panthers, boars, wolves, dogs, gazelles, hares. But we are particularly struck by the *bestiarii,* men who fought for their lives against wild animals. The tomb shows a young *bestiarius.* He is attacking a panther attached to a bull by a rope, which seems to restrict the panther's movement somewhat. One panel shows an athlete at grips with a bull, whose side he has just pierced with his lance.

The hunt offered a variety of pleasures. Sometimes deer were unleashed; the audience were allowed into the arena, and could take away with them any animals they could kill; sometimes well-armed gladiators, skilled in all an animal's tricks, were able to kill the animals they were fighting without too much difficulty. Sometimes prisoners were sent into the arena. They were armed to defend themselves, but unused to this sort of combat, paralyzed by fear, sure of being torn to pieces by lions and tigers, they thought it a release to be able to kill themselves rather than serve as living fodder for wild beasts.

Sculptures, paintings and graffiti show clearly enough that gladiatorial bouts were the Pompeians' great passion.

What was the origin of this slaughter of unhappy men, who, not wanting to die, killed each other for the amusement of the crowd?

Gladiatorial bouts were introduced by Junius Brutus, and it was not until some thousand years later, in 401, that the Emperor Honorius had the courage to abolish them. The ancient Romans considered the massacre of captives on the tomb of those who had died to be a sacred duty—an appeasement of the *manes.* But such butchery came to be considered revolting. Instead of killing defenceless prisoners, they were given arms to kill each other, and the lives of those who had killed the most were spared.

The taste for slaughter grew, so that it was not enough to stage bouts only in celebration of funerals; they were held on every

Boar attacked by dogs (group discovered in Pompeii).

"Wealthy citizens commonly left a legacy for the holding of an annual combat to celebrate the anniversary of their deaths." —Below: Victor and victim. Right: Fresco depicting a bout.

occasion, including banquets. They were carefully organized spectacles, pleasures paid for by affluence to flatter the mob.

Gladiators were brought up in their trade from childhood. They were trained for killing, specially fed and clothed; the fight had more interest when the combatants were of equal strength. The advertisements in Pompeii show the number of gladiators in pairs: twenty pairs, thirty pairs.

The stucco bas-reliefs, once brightly coloured, which embellish the tomb of Scaurus depict the details of these bloody scenes. Two rivals are on horseback; they have lowered the visors of their helmets; they are armed with lances and round shields. One is called Brebix, the other Nobilior. They were famous fighters, who have proved their skill and courage. One has won fifteen bouts, the other eleven. Two retired gladiators, who have been victors in thirty fights, watch the contest leaning on a huge shield. Normally, the competitors were on foot; only the first round took place on horseback.

Next to the panel representing the beginning of a bout is one which shows the end of the fight. One of the gladiators, half naked and lightly armed, has lost after sixteen successful combats. There is a gaping wound in his chest, and his failing grasp has let go his shield. His lance lies on the ground, and his enemy has his foot over it. The wounded man admits that he is beaten, and turns to the crowd, begging for his life; he raises his left hand to ask for mercy. The victor, who has just won his fifth fight, is a heavily armed warrior; he waits for the audience to give its verdict. He is not allowed to spare his victim; this is a privilege that belongs to the people or the Emperor. Julius Caesar would generally spare the gladiators; his cruel successors did not always share his taste for clemency. The crowd replied to the pleas of the victim with a gesture, which was a real life-and-death judgement. A raised thumb meant death; thumb hidden in a closed fist was life.

The modest Vestal Virgins could often be the most pitiless of the spectators. They were amongst the first to give an unfavourable verdict in order to savour the horrible pleasure of watching a man die a graceful death!

It seems that it was difficult to appeal to the Pompeians' tender feelings.

When the popular verdict had been given, the victim had to present the spot chosen by the victor for the fatal blow, without averting his eyes.

The death blow has been struck; the victim dies. An official dressed as Mercury makes sure of the death by applying a red hot iron. The body is then dragged out on an iron hook through the death gate by slaves, and thrown on a charnel heap.

In another group a gladiator has dropped his shield, a shameful mistake. He flees; his adversary pursues him, and his victory will be easy.

Finally, a panel above the tomb shows a wounded gladiator; the victor makes ready to kill him. But the *lanista,* leader of the gladiator, holds him back until the people have decided.

Gladiators varied their tactics to amuse the crowd. The bloodiest bouts were the most exciting. As the struggle grew fiercer, and dying warriors fell on the sand, the crowd's tender feelings were submerged in a lust for death; they became like wild beasts who grow dangerous after tasting blood. Slaves and slaughtered prisoners were no longer enough; even women were made to perform as gladiators! And some stars of the arena, maddened by blood lust, dazzled by the prospect of the prizes offered to the victor to frenetic applause, wanted only to fight, strike, kill in a homicidal fury.

Mosaic found on a doorstep, near the Marine gate: fight scene.

Maps showing Vesuvius erupting.

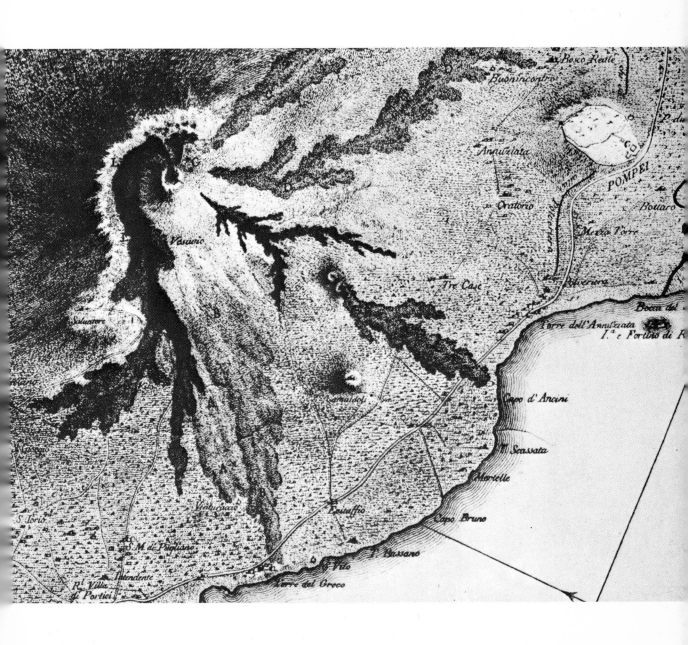

Aerial view of Vesuvius (modern photograph).

8 - The death of Pompeii

Venus, the guardian of Pompeii, in fact protected the town particularly badly. Nearby Vesuvius was to become the avenging angel of the town of pleasure.

The volcano had already given a terrible warning. On 5th February, 63 AD, a terrible eruption devastated the area. Here is how Seneca described it:

"Pompeii, a considerable town in Campania, was overwhelmed by an earthquake, which affected the surrounding country. This happened in winter, a season which our forefathers tell us is normally protected against such events... Though there had been several alerts, Campania had in fact never been affected by earthquake. The only tribute it paid to the scourge was fear; but this time it was cruelly struck. Apart from Pompeii, Herculaneum was partly destroyed, and what remains is not safe... In Naples, many individual houses were knocked down, but public buildings remain standing. Villas were shaken, but they suffered no other damage. It is said that a flock of six hundred sheep were killed, statues overturned, and that many unhappy individuals were found wandering about the countryside, fear having made them lose their reason!"

But this was only a prelude to the appalling trials the unfortunate town was to suffer. The details of the last and final catastrophe are related by Pliny the Younger in a letter to Tacitus:

"You have asked me for details of my uncle's death, so that you can leave an accurate record of it for posterity.

"My uncle was stationed at Misenum, in active command of the fleet. On the ninth day before the Kalends of September, in the early afternoon, my mother drew his attention to a cloud of unusual size and appearance. He had been out in the sun, had taken a cold bath, and lunched while lying down, and was then working at his books. He called for his sandals and climbed up to a spot which would give him a better view of what was happening. It was not clear from which mountain the cloud was rising—it was afterwards known to be Vesuvius. Its general appearance was rather like that of a tree, and particularly a pine, for it rose to a great height on a trunk, splitting into branches. Perhaps this was because it was thrust upwards by the first blast and then left unsupported as the pressure subsided, and perhaps, too, it was borne down by its own weight and gradually dispersed. Sometimes it looked white, sometimes blotched and dirty, depending on whether it was carrying off soil or ashes.

"The phenomenon aroused my uncle's scientific curiosity, and he decided to examine it more closely... As he was leaving the house he was handed a message from Rectina, wife of Tascus. Alarmed by the imminence of the danger (for her house was at the foot of the mountain, so that escape was only possible by boat) she implored him to rescue her. He therefore

changed his plans, and what was begun in a spirit of enquiry he completed as a hero. He ordered the warships to be got ready, and went on board himself to help Rectina and many other people who lived on the shores of this lovely coast.

"He hurried to the place which everyone else was fleeing; he sailed straight into danger, his hand on the tiller. He was entirely fearless, describing each new movement and phase of the portent to be noted down exactly as he observed them.

"Ashes were already falling, hotter and thicker as the ships drew near, followed by bits of pumice and blackened stones, charred and cracked by the flames; then suddenly they were in shallow water, and the shore was blocked by debris from the mountain. My uncle considered turning back; but he said to the pilot: 'Fortune favours courage: make for Pomponianus!' He was at Stabiae, cut off on the other side of a small bay formed by the gradual curve of the shore. He was not yet in direct danger, though this was immanent as the devastation spread. He had already brought all his belongings on board ship, and was only waiting for the contrary wind to die down before setting off. This wind was blowing in my uncle's favour, and he was able to bring his ship in. He embraced his friend, and was able to cheer and encourage him... Meanwhile broad sheets of fire and leaping flames blazed at several points, their glare emphasized by the darkness of the night. My uncle tried to

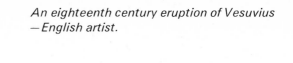
*An eighteenth century eruption of Vesuvius
—English artist.*

reassure his companions by telling them that these were empty houses on fire abandoned by the peasants in terror. Then he went to rest, and clearly he slept soundly, for he was a stout man, and his breathing was rather loud and heavy and could be heard by people coming and going outside his door. But by this time the courtyard which gave access to his bedroom was full of ashes mixed with pumice stones. If he had stayed much longer, it would have been impossible to get him out. He was wakened, and he left his room to join Pomponianus and the others who were already about. They debated whether to stay indoors or take their chance in the open, for the buildings were now shaking with violent shocks, and seemed to be torn from their foundations as they were rocked to and fro. Outside, on the other hand, there was the danger of falling pumice stones, even though these were light and porous. Of the two dangers, they chose the latter... As a protection against falling objects they put pillows on their heads, held in place with cloths.

"Elsewhere day was dawning, but for them it was still the blackest night, which they relieved by lighting torches and various sorts of lamps. It was decided to go down to the coast, to see whether there was any possibility of escape by sea; but the waves were still wild and dangerous. At this my uncle lay down on a stretched-out sheet. He asked for cold water, and drank a couple of times. Then the smell of sulphur which was

a warning of the nearness of danger drove everyone to flight, and forced my uncle to stand up. He stood leaning on two slaves, and suddenly collapsed dead."

Pliny wrote a second letter to Tacitus, who was anxious to have as many details as possible:

"By now it was dawn, but the light was still dim and faint. The buildings around us were already tottering, and the open space we were in was too small for us not to be in real danger if the house collapsed. We finally decided to leave town. We were followed by a panic-stricken mob—as happens in such situations, people prefer to act on anyone's decision but their own. Once we were out of town, we stopped, but new terrors awaited us. The carriages which we had brought with us began to run in all directions, although the ground was quite level. They would not remain in one place even when wedged with stones. The sea appeared to be sucked back on itself and backed off from the shore by the earthquake. At any rate, the shore extended further, and a great many fish were stranded on the sands. On the other side a frightful black cloud, torn by bursts of flame, parted to reveal great tongues of fire, like vast flashes of lightning... The cloud sank down to earth and covered the sea. It hid the Isle of Capri and blotted out the promontory of Misenum...

"Ashes were already falling, though not yet quickly. I looked behind me, to see a

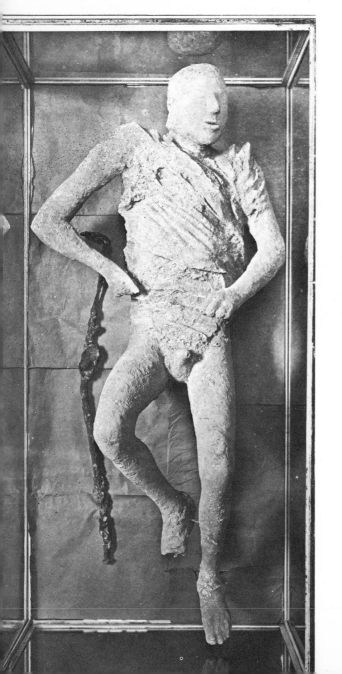

thick black cloud coming up fast, spreading over the earth like a flood. "Let us leave the road while we can still see', I said to my mother, "or we shall be knocked down and trampled under foot in the dark by the crowd behind us." We had hardly stopped before the darkness thickened. This was not the dark of a cloudy, moonless night; it was the blackness of a room in which all the lights had gone out. We could hear women crying, children howling, men shouting. Someone was calling out for his father, another for his son, another for his wife; they were trying to recognize each other by the sounds of their voices. Some were concerned about their own fate; others about that of their relatives. There were those who prayed for death in their terror of dying. Many sought the aid of the gods, but still more were convinced that there were no gods left, and that the universe was plunged into darkness for ever more. Many, too, added to the real dangers by inventing imaginary fears. Some said that part of Misenum had collapsed, or that another part was on fire, and these false reports were believed.

"A gleam of light appeared, but we took this not for the return of daylight but as a warning of the approaching flames. However, the flames remained some distance off; then darkness returned, and the shower of ash grew heavier and thicker than before. We rose from time to time and shook off the cinders, which would otherwise have crushed and buried us. I could boast that not a

"Some bravely faced the death they believed to be inevitable. We find them stretched out in attitudes of resignation."— Left: Corpse found in Pompeii.

Opposite: Tacitus, the historian. Pliny the Younger described the catastrophe in a letter to him.

Below: A corpse discovered near Nola gate.

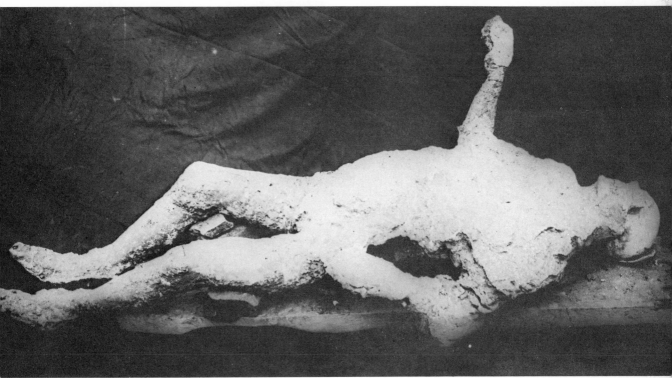

*"It happened on 23rd November 79...
Several historians tell us that at the moment disaster struck the Pompeians were
enjoying themselves in the Amphitheatre...
More women have been discovered
amongst the dead than men."* Moulds
of the corpses of a man and a woman.

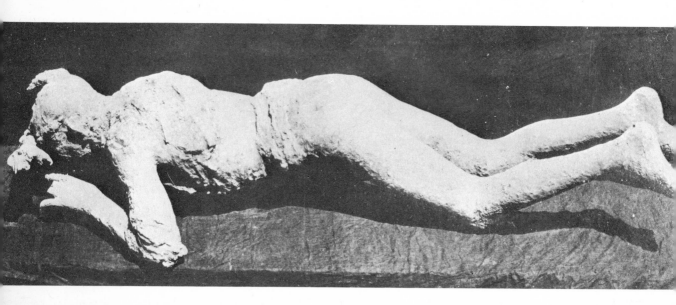

groan or a sigh of fear escaped me; but I was consoled by the dreadful yet comforting thought that the universe was dying with me, and I with it."

In fact, the universe was not yet to die; but three towns, Pompeii, Stabiae and Herculaneum disappeared at that moment. Seneca had died in 65 AD, and the final catastrophe was in 79 AD.

We know the day of the eruption and the disappearance of Pompeii. It was 23rd November 79. Bonucci is prepared to be precise: he gives the time as one o'clock in the afternoon.

Several authors say that at the time of the tragedy the Pompeians were enjoying a performance in the amphitheatre. This theory, which provides a basis for moral-drawing, relies on the authority of Dion Cassius. But on the details of what actually happened modern writers are better informed than contemporary sources. The excavation of the town has revealed all the details of its final moments.

Pompeii did not die a sudden death under torrents of flame erupting from the depths of Vesuvius. The volcano gave plenty of warning: a rain of ash and *lapilli,* pumice fragments, fell slowly over a wide area. The Pompeians had time to take to flight.

Many died in panic, and several rushed to meet the death they thought they were fleeing. Farmers from the surrounding fields ran towards the town to seek refuge within its strong walls; the townsmen ran into the fields to escape falling masonry. Several skeletons have been found under the ruins of collapsed columns and walls. One Pompeian was crushed by an equestrian statue of Nero which fell from the triumphal arch on Minerva Street. Animals refused to move, petrified with fear, or stampeded into the night. The remains of a goat which had hidden in a stove have been discovered; skeletons of dogs and horses have also been found. There is no trace of cats; their survival instinct seems to have been particularly strong.

The Pompeian men did not know what to do. Some, beside themselves, rushed about aimlessly; others faced up to the dangers, and tried to open a passageway through heaps of lava with axes. Then there were those who bravely faced the death they believed to be inevitable. We find them stretched out in attitudes of resignation. The soldier, as a worthy Roman warrior, died faithfully at his post. Sixty-three skeletons were found in the barracks.

More women than men have been found amongst the dead. The wife and mother preferred to die rather than survive alone. A desperate mother, fleeing towards Nola with her son in her arms and her two daughters close behind, is preserved in the ash. Their fine earrings and gold bracelets shaped like serpents tell us they were wealthy people.

Women are more attached than men to personal possessions; many of them tried

It happened 23rd November 79...

to take their gold and jewels with them. Several died trying to save their caskets and jewel cases. The volcano would not wait for ever, even if it seemed ready to give the inhabitants time to leave. Sometimes Vesuvius carried off the very things that the Pompeians most wanted to keep from it. We find a bonework basket containing gold, silver and bronze coins, two pairs of earrings shaped like orange segments, and a cornelian ringstone showing a chariot drawn by two stags and driven by a winged god. Wrapped in cloth, and carefully packed in a large cauldron which could be easily carried, was a superb group of Bacchus and Ampelus in bronze set with silver.

During these dreadful events some believed, as we have seen, that the world was at an end; others hoped that the rain of ash would soon pass, like a shower of hail falling on crops. Some looked for refuge on the upper terraces, thinking that the lava would not reach so high. The remains of eleven Pompeians were discovered on the first floor of a house on Stabiae Street. They had brought their money and jewels with them, and while they anxiously watched the lava rising below, the roof, shaken by a violent quake, collapsed on top of them. Others hid in closed rooms, crypts, or underground cellars. Diomedes's cellar is particularly well known. There, surrounded by huge wine jars, the remains of seventeen people were discovered. A young girl fell dying into the ash—the shape of her beautiful body has been preserved. The hardened lava showing the outline of the young beauty's breast is one of the most famous exhibits in the Naples museum.

The most terrible fate was reserved for those who had the misfortune to find cellars solid enough to resist all tremors. Buried alive, they died of hunger. In one such cellar were found scattered human remains and the skeleton of an animal; we can guess what happened. A man had sheltered there with his dog to wait until the storm passed. Then, when he decided to leave, he found that the volcano had blocked every exit. His voice was unheard from the depths of the vault. No ray of light reached him. He died first. The dog, desperately hungry, ate his corpse, of which only a few bones remain. Finally, it was the animal's turn to die.

Seeing the shapes of these men from another time, mummified by the eruption, is a

Left: A dog...

137

moving experience; it makes us pause to think. These moulds of the Pompeians provide details about the catastrophe, and tell us a great deal about the men of the ancient world. The clothes of the victims are so perfectly preserved by the lava that we can make out the textures of the different cloths—it is almost as though one could reach out and take the fine clothes off the naked flesh. The skulls and human remains which have been found have been carefully studied. The skulls are of three basic shapes, which indicates that there were different races in Pompeii; but it is clear that the basic shape and size of men and animals have not changed over the centuries.

Has physical beauty deteriorated? This is a subject which has not been scientifically studied. Lord Hamilton, English ambassador at the end of the eighteenth century, claims that the teeth of Pompeian ladies were more beautiful than those of his contemporaries. He attributes the change to eating sweets, which were unknown in antiquity.

As we see each day's excavations unveil new discoveries, it seems surprising that they began so late, for although they were started over two hundred years ago, they are not yet complete.

Why did it take so long to uncover a town which was known to be full of treasure? The Pompeians were naturally anxious to recover their belongings as soon as the storm had passed. But their houses were buried under a thick layer of lava.

The excavations reveal the efforts which were made by the survivors to recover the images of their household gods, to dig out their jewelry, and save their loved ones from the tomb.

The danger of landslides, the extreme looseness of the soil, noxious gases and the stench of corpses must have alarmed and discouraged many.

Titus thought of using the estates of those who had died without heirs to reconstruct the towns destroyed by Vesuvius. He died too soon to put his scheme into effect, and the Pompeians sought a safer refuge.

Vesuvius, from a mural in the centurion's house.—Following page: A cultivated field, at Pompeii, so far unexcavated. Vesuvius is in the background.

Index

Photos : Alinari/Giraudon : 11, 20b, 36b, 37b, 39, 49, 50, 52, 54, 55, 57, 62, 64, 65, 67, 68, 69, 92, 93, 98, 104, 113b, 120a, 136 — Anderson/Giraudon : 16, 47, 66, 134b — Anderson/Viollet : 31b, 34, 105, 109 — Archives : 15, 20a, 23, 24, 26b, 27, 31a, 32b, 35, 40, 56, 76, 87a, b, 91a, b, 106, 114, 120c, 125, 130, 133a, 138 — Brogi-Giraudon : 19, 46, 53, 70, 102 — Enit : end papers, 6, 8, 10, 13, 29, 32a, 45, 58a, 72, 74, 117b, 118, 126 — Giraudon : 61, 100, 103, 127 — Harlingue : 85 — Lauros/Giraudon : 12, 80, 101 — Viollet : 2, 18a, b, c, 20c, 21, 22, 26a, 28, 36a, 37a, 41, 42, 43, 44, 58b, 60, 63, 71, 73, 79, 81, 82, 83, 84, 88, 95, 96, 111, 113a, 117a, 120b, 123, 128, 132, 133b, 134a, 140.

Depósito legal B. 36632-1972   Printer, industria gráfica sa
Tuset, 19 Barcelona   San Vicente dels Horts   1972

Printed in Spain